SpringerBriefs in Business

More information about this series at https://link.springer.com/bookseries/8860

Andrea Pecorale

Essence of the PET Radiopharmaceutical Business

A Practical Guide

 Springer

Andrea Pecorale
Crescentino, Vercelli, Italy

ISSN 2191-5482   ISSN 2191-5490   (electronic)
SpringerBriefs in Business
ISBN 978-3-030-97936-2   ISBN 978-3-030-97937-9   (eBook)
https://doi.org/10.1007/978-3-030-97937-9

This Springer imprint is published by the registered company Springer Nature Switzerland AG
The registered company address is: Gewerbestrasse 11, 6330 Cham, Switzerland

To my mother and father and their example

Preface: What Are We Talking About? What This Book Considers and What It Does Not

The idea of writing a book on PET radiopharmaceuticals has crossed my mind for some time, ever since I crossed the threshold of 50 years.

Since 2014, I no longer directly follow a production site in its routine, managing staff.

In the course of my subsequent and current job, in which I carry out a coordination activity between several PET manufacturing sites, I have often heard from elderly colleagues, in light of the requests I made to third-party sites and the timing that I envisaged, that I was losing sensitivity of what actually a production site can or cannot easily do.

It is also for this reason that I started to write my memories and reflections. Unfortunately, time is not a good friend in this sense. It is possible, I hope, that the points raised by me as problems have already been largely resolved in the current productive world.

This book will neither draw up nor consider a detailed list of what current regulations allow, or not allow, in the various areas of radiopharmaceutical production (e.g. classified environments, radiation protection, good manufacturing practice [GMP]). All this information is well reported in the literature.

My intention is to navigate the reader in some organizational and logistical aspects of the 'industrial' world of radiopharmaceuticals, which I was able to deal with from 28 years of direct experience. The opinions I express in the various chapters derive from my way of operating in different situations and, in many cases, from the colleagues I was lucky enough to meet. My experience developed in Italy but then extends to the whole of Europe, with some contacts in the US and Asian radiopharmaceutical markets.

The book begins with a short section on what I believe are the best personal aptitudes to be successful in the world of radiopharmaceuticals. I agree that it is anomalous that personal attitudes can be linked to such a highly automated sector, but this is my thought:

Unfortunately, I do not have any truth.

The opinions I express in the various chapters derive from my way of operating in different situations and, in many cases, from the colleagues I was lucky enough to meet.

My experience developed in Italy but then also extended to the whole of Europe, with some contacts in the US and Asian radiopharmaceutical markets.

The book begins with a short section on what I believe are the best personal aptitudes to be successful in the world of radiopharmaceuticals.

I agree that it is anomalous that personal attitudes can be linked to such a highly automated sector, but this is my thought.

We then move on to the production part, with an introduction to the concept of financial profitability and to the two types of production: direct, through a production site operating entirely under its own responsibility, and indirect, in which production is carried out by third-party sites commonly referred to as CMOs (contract manufacturer organizations).

Since the production sites, in some cases, are varied and not all in their own territory, I have included a section on the management of a PET network.

At the end of some chapters, sometimes even at the end of some of the paragraphs, I have included short stories. The stories fit into the context of my personal experience, and names and locations have been changed or not mentioned at all (in respect of the unwitting protagonists) and have the purpose, or rather the hope, of making the understanding of the theoretical introductory part more immediate.

I believe that some of the considerations mentioned in this book can be applied not only to PET, but to all radiopharmaceuticals; however, on this point, I leave the reader to judge.

Crescentino, Italy   Andrea Pecorale

Contents

Chapter 1
Personal Attitudes to Approach the Production of Radiopharmaceuticals: Are You Always Inclined to Do This Job? Employee and Consultant

Abstract The author focuses his attention on the selection of personnel and consultant in a radiopharmaceutical plant, at operational, non-operational, and managerial levels and to retain the developed competences.

Keywords Hiring process · Education · Placement at work · Working shifts · Team building

Employee

Is there an aptitude, a predisposition, to work in the production of radiopharmaceuticals?

I would like to be able to say that the reason why I started dealing with radiopharmaceuticals was a deliberate choice, dictated by the real interest in this sector, perhaps gained in the first years of university studies.

In reality it was, like many things in life, a completely random event.

In my fourth year of university, like many of my colleagues, I found myself in the position of having to choose the discipline, better to say the laboratory (the thesis was experimental) in which to develop the thesis.

Given the high number of requests, my generation born of the boom of the 60s had no problems in terms of numbers, I was struggling a bit in research.

A subtle sense of anxiety did not help, many colleagues had already found their 'place' in the most popular laboratories.

I still remember, it seems to me a spring morning, the handwritten leaflet hanging on the bulletin board, in which a radiopharmaceutical laboratory about to be established was mentioned. After a short interview, I began my thesis activities.

The laboratory was poor in equipment, almost non-existent, but certainly full of good intentions and innovative ideas.

Looking the past with the current eyes, with the experience gained, I can say that this was the first successful project in which, in spite of any preliminary feasibility analysis, I actually participated. In short, a first test of patience and perseverance.

You can see that it is difficult to talk about 'aptitude' to do this job when the author of the book admits the causality of being in this environment, but over the years I have had the opportunity to work in already consolidated heterogeneous groups, to create new ones myself and to 'observe' operational groups in different manufacturing sites.

Hence, my presumption in wanting to provide some suggestions.

I am not a professional in personnel selection, so my way of presenting will appear unusual, but it considers my direct experience.

Working in a PET radiopharmaceutical production environment requires being few.

The economic sustainability of the production site requires a limited number of employees, despite having to comply with the same rules as the 'classic' pharmaceutical.

Furthermore, the spaces are almost always very small, compatible with small production volumes.

I remember an important supplier of plastic components who, faced with my request to develop caps for vials in a number that seemed consistent to me, we were talking about a thousand vials a year, asked me if I did some modeling.

The same logic applies to the number of employees.

For each department manager, Production, Quality Control (QC), Maintenance, Quality Assurance (QA), we can consider some technician or operator, but let us forget that we have dozens of people for each single department.

A considerable degree of independence and autonomy is therefore always envisaged for each employee, as it is possible that in each single department they can also work alone.

In light of this degree of independence, it is therefore necessary to think about a very accurate training, which considers not only the technical bases of the activities that take place in the facility, obviously combined with the GMP and radiation protection aspects, but also with a true coaching with experienced colleagues, which in my opinion cannot be less than three months.

This is the fundamental reason why the selection must be careful, on both sides!

It is necessary to explain in detail what we ask for, and it is essential that the candidate spends at least one day in the manufacturing facility before being hired.

In the moment of selection, the first point on which we discuss is schooling.

In light of the need to interface with complex issues, fully automated production, GMPs, radiation protection, and knowledge of English, the 'temptation' is to aim for very high school profiles.

This approach, in principle, is not wrong, but it is necessary to evaluate what are the growth opportunities for the candidate.

A high profile is a demanding profile.

In the case of operational personnel, routine activities, in the first steps of their career, with their 'atypical' corollary of nocturnal production or radioactivity management, will be a phenomenal attraction.

But over time, let us say after one or at most two years, the first signs of fatigue will begin, if we are not able to propose new activities compared to those already carried out.

Radiation can attract and generate excessive 'confidence', often more verbal than substance.

In this regard, I quote the rite of my 'first contamination'.

First job immediately after university: after the first ritual training, I began with caution to handle small amounts of isotopes for simple labelling.

Being research activities carried out mostly in glove boxes, despite the precious advice of the chemical expert who followed me, with thirty years of experience, I ended up contaminating my hands and the sleeves of my coat.

I only noticed it at the exit, which was very close to the laboratory, when the radiation detector began to 'croak' with an ever-higher frequency.

As the radiation protection technician takes the necessary measurements and I move between the metre and the sink, a buzz begins to rise.

Initially, I did not notice it, both because I must admit I felt nervous in that new situation and because the area was very busy.

But after a few minutes, I realize that there are at least a dozen colleagues who in unison begin to clap their hands and congratulate me: by contaminating me, I officially became part of the family.

Normally, the team, in addition to being small, is also relatively young, and this point facilitates the insertion of new hires.

I have also always found in the world of radiopharmaceuticals a low level of competitiveness, in its most negative sense.

On this last point I have always thought that, given the concentration required by work, there is not even time for these amenities.

In defining the candidate's profile, the saying goes: 'just as good as required'.

The first obstacle to overcome is that of the manager.

The reason is simple: in addition to what we ask the candidate to do, there are a lot of other things we could get them to do more. But often, in my experience, it happens that the things we ask to do are already more than enough to cover a working day, so the things that 'we could' do more inevitably remain suspended.

A lower level of education, I am thinking of the high school diploma, provides greater guarantees in terms of loyalty to the company.

Regarding the age of a candidate for operational roles, some of my personal considerations, which obviously do not constitute a rule.

All candidates, regardless of gender and age, are perfectly eligible for this role, but my reflection is based on sustainability, on the 'retention' of the resource in the company.

The young figures are obviously the most 'attractive', full of enthusiasm and desire to do, and they fit into the context and bring joy and lightheartedness.

But life in the PET manufacturing site is not easy.

Problems must, if possible, be resolved immediately.

For scheduled maintenance it is often used on weekends. This means that a working day, in case of problems, can easily exceed the normal eight hours.

In the case of production problems, the need to make radioactivity decay means that the intervention must be performed, if we imagine the nocturnal and early morning production, in the late afternoon if not in the evening, close to the next production.

This limits the possibility for an employee to plan their life.

Furthermore, due to the specific skills that develop in the departments and the reduced availability of personnel, it is not easy to delegate activities among the various employees. A colleague employed by the European Community told me, it was the early 2000s, that in a PET congress in Finland a friend of him, on hearing the news that he would soon be involved in an industrial PET production, had warned him that the cyclotron (but here I think he was referring to the whole PET process) was a real divorce machine.

So, returning to the figure of the young candidate, the PET experience can be in contrast with an active social life, with aperitifs, travels.

It should also be considered that 'on-call availability' is a fundamental element not only for maintenance but also for the operational aspects of the life of the manufacturing site. Additions and cancellations of doses, transport organizational problems require continuous contact with the site.

The writer was contacted on Christmas day by a hospital that had forgotten to place an order and, in different years, always on the same holiday, I had to arrange for a technician to be sent to a third-party site that had problems in guaranteeing the production.

More mature figures, therefore less 'tempted' by leisure and social life, can give a greater guarantee of sustainability over time of this rhythm of life.

In my experience, the best 'performance' was provided by colleagues a little older in age, perhaps with grown-up children.

In this case, the employee's attention can certainly be attracted by the solidity of the work and also by the significant economic benefits that derive from it.

The two age groups, if well harmonized with each other, constitute a disruptive driving force for the facility.

The intellectual vivacity of the young employee and the wisdom of the elderly dilute each other, allowing us to have ideas that are then actually viable.

Given the complexity and potential criticality of the issues addressed (drug plus radioactivity), it is in fact appropriate that this mixture is always present and that neither of them prevails over the other.

A too young team, in my opinion, can jeopardize the company's production continuity, in light of the fact that technicians often work at night with great autonomy.

The reflection also applies to those with managerial responsibilities. My suggestion is to embrace solutions only after comparing yourself with older colleagues, regardless of hierarchical relationships.

It is a practice that is valid not only for technical problems but also for organizational and disciplinary ones.

Let us not forget that we always talk about very small teams: an error of analysis and intervention on the staff would have an immediate impact and not easy to recover over time.

In one of my experiences in an operations department, I was always supported from the two older employees.

Their advice, which I still remember, in addition to allowing them to value themselves as people, has always allowed me, even when my final decision was in contrast with the suggestions received, to have a broader view of my actions.

I have always shied away from using the term 'family' for a PET department. I think the comparison is inappropriate and excessive.

I have always preferred to stimulate the idea of a group of 'minds', professionals, at the service of health.

But due to the fact that there are few of them, this comes close to the idea of a family, it is necessary to work in a regime of total transparency and sharing of information, respecting diversity.

Here, more than a family, I tried to develop the idea of the orchestra. Each of us knows how to use a specific instrument, which corresponds to personal talent, but no one alone can provide the final result that only an orchestra can give.

To share information, I recommend setting a morning 'point', of about 30, at the junction between the two shifts (night and day). This is to allow also and above all to those who work at night to be always updated and vice versa.

And the 'point' is performed by eating a hearty breakfast together, especially when things went badly at night. Because everyone is able to celebrate when things are going well!

I mention a case that happened to me, in my youth, I had been working in the company for a couple of years.

An operator was often restless and showed indifference towards colleagues.

Partly from a personal nature, partly because at that time I was carrying out social service experiences, I had taken the trouble to try to help him by making him speak and, as far as possible, giving suggestions.

On the occasion of one of our chats, in light of the fact that the issues raised seemed so repetitive to me that they bordered on a sort of self-satisfaction in feeling a victim of events, unfortunately, I advanced the suggestion to get help with psychological support.

After a couple of days, the operator gave me a letter, written by his lawyer and with a copy of the management of the company where I worked, in which I was thanked for the suggestion and covertly, if I remember correctly, doubts were raised about my effective personnel management skills.

As the reader can imagine, it got me a rough time.

I think I was able to keep the job thanks to the understanding of the management and in the light of my short work experience.

It is therefore difficult for me now to even think about the idea of family in a work environment.

Still in the context of operational roles, in terms of education, the figure of a graduate and/or in possession of a scientific bachelor's degree was the one who provided the best results. Although in distant times, when the production of radiopharmaceuticals had recently been assimilated to pharmaceuticals, I was able to meet zealous and perfect operators even in possession of a middle and even elementary licence.

But in today's world, production and quality control machines are so interfaced with management software that a minimum of IT training and knowledge of the English language are essential.

Not to mention that, often, the manuals of the equipment are in English like the internal communications themselves, in the case of a multinational company.

But do not look for excellence in this, it is not necessary.

Above all, look for the following qualities: education, calmness of mind, and a certain 'perspicacity' in identifying possible solutions.

It is a good rule for me, during selective interviews, to present a concrete case to the attention of the candidate, whether it is of a technical nature or related to any relational problems with colleagues or supervisors and ask how it would behave and what solutions it would propose to the company.

It is not important that the candidate knows the peculiarity of PET production, even if for specific needs it can be a 'nice to have', what interests us is precisely the level of insight. What they does not know they will learn with time, perseverance, and colleagues.

Avoid like the plague from overly 'decision-making' figures, remember the small team, but prefer the figures oriented towards a progressive approach in actions and aimed at negotiation and compromise. They will be very useful in the reality in which it will have to operate.

I myself, lacking any technical expertise on automatic radiopharmaceutical production systems, spent the first two years of my career working on an automatic machine for the production of 131I Iodine capsules, a prototype that never had worked.

But with enormous patience and countless 'escape' attempts to get me assigned desk tasks (promptly rejected by my first boss, who I must admit knew a lot about training), working closely with an expert maintenance technician (to whom I owe the maxims on how to live in the company), the manufacturer, and the workers, I managed to make the equipment works by gathering a wealth of experience and relational skills with suppliers that are still useful today.

Once I have identified the possible candidate or candidates, my suggestion is to invite them to spend some time, even better if an entire day, within the manufacturing facility, assigning it to one or more technicians.

It is essential that the candidates see the environments in which will operate, which are often narrow, and that they are also introduced to the need for attention in handling radioactive material.

It is also advisable that the same has the opportunity to verify, especially in production, the need to lift weights (shielded containers), an activity that must be within their reach, being frequent in the production field.

Radioactivity, as already mentioned, exerts a certain attraction, rather than fear, I think dictated by curiosity and by the known events of nuclear disasters. But it is necessary to reiterate to the candidate that, even if low, the danger exists.

I once selected a young chemistry graduate.

On his first day on the job, employed in the Mo99/Tc99m generator production department, they came to hastily call me because he had escaped from the department. They found him huddled in a corner. He had not been involved in any incident, simply the fear suddenly appeared, which had not emerged in any way during the interviews.

This is why it is important that, even if briefly, before making the choice, the candidate can actually know the work environment.

The possibility must also be accepted, which often happens in PET departments, that work takes place in environments without natural light and that the atmosphere is in strong 'depression' compared to the external environment. A full day in these conditions can also be difficult to endure.

Also collect information about the visit from your technicians. The more the choice is shared with them, the easier it will be to insert the employee later.

In the case of selection of responsible (managerial) person, the same 'recommendations' as the point dedicated to technicians apply to me.

Do not seek the super-expert, except of course if you need them, but the ability to judge, moderate and without extremes. They will find themselves guiding people who will technically know much more than them, and the main task will be to harmonize the activities in the departments, calming the minds, if necessary.

In the case of production sites belonging to multinational groups, their role will also be that of transferring the central Corporate directives, enhancing their possible points of benefit. Directives that, in my experience, are never easily accepted, given that there is always the belief, not always wrongly, of operating locally already in the best of systems.

Even for a responsible candidate, the 'tour' system in the facility applies. If possible, in this case, it is even more important than for a technical candidate.

However, the personal opinion of employees on the candidate does not affect much.

As much it turns out to be frank for a future candidate, their colleague, so much it turns out to be 'censored' in the case of a candidate with roles of responsibility.

Placement at Work

Technical Assistant

I suggest taking the first two weeks for a complete technical training, what is referred to in jargon as 'induction training'.

The temptation to 'enter the field' is strong both for the new employee but also and above all for colleagues: let us hold back!

It is necessary to read and understand the key documents of the facility, from the Site Master File, to the VMP, to the procedural system and the radiation protection standards, accompanied by a verification of the actual understanding of the same through small tests. A brief interview with company functions is essential, not just those more specifically related to the life of the PET facility (QA, RA, production, and QC, radiation protection and conventional safety).

It is useful for the candidate to know the functioning and operating methods of ancillary functions, such as Customer Service, logistics, marketing, finance, and the purchasing department.

This is to allow the new technician to better understand the environment in which they work and the nature/origin of the various requests that they will receive, sometimes in an excited way, during their activity.

Understanding the needs of customers and having a minimum view of the financial picture make the employee responsible, making them feel part and in some way 'protagonist' of the life of the manufacturing site.

For practical training, the new employee should have a 'tutor' among the technicians, with whom to initially assist in all phases of the process, both production and QC, practically without carrying out any activity.

At least two weeks, holding back the temptation to get your hands on it.

Afterwards, in the following weeks, the new technician gradually accesses the simpler stages of processing, always accompanied by the tutor.

Three months is the minimum time for practical training, before being able to actually act independently.

If possible, use the opportunity of 'test' work, in order to actually measure the ability of the new employee.

Inserting a new person correctly is a great effort, of resources and of time. But it is with this investment that the foundations are laid both to avoid operational problems but also to create that 'bond' with the PET manufacturing site, which is, as it actually is, a concentrate of professionalism at the service of health.

Collaborator in a Non-operational Role

A situation that I have faced in recent years, confronted with the need to manage multiple sites, is that of having a financial analyst next to me, a 'business analyst'.

In this sense I have had experienced collaborators, with previous long financial experience in the industrial world, but also young people, with very little experience.

In both cases, however, the problem arose of 'introducing them' to the specificity of the topic.

In fact, it is difficult for me to think that there could be an analysis of this type without fully grasping, for example, the difficulty of being able to guarantee production continuity and a business that, however optimal, must include:

(a) A production reliability of at least 95%
(b) The need to have to stop the activities due to unexpected and expensive maintenance, for GMP or radiation protection needs

(c) Having to be in a position to produce at a loss, especially after the resumption of production following periods of plant shutdown that had a heavy impact on customers (a lack of supplies for long periods of time)

(d) Having to program technical batches, which are expensive for the use of personnel and the consumption of raw materials.

How to train a PET economist?

Surely by providing a general technical basis not only on the process but also, and above all, on the GMP aspects and supporting radiation protection without which it is not clear why the operational choices are made. At least a couple of weeks, also ideal with a discussion with function managers.

It is also not to be underestimated to follow at least a couple of productions.

Whether the business analyst follows one or more sites, I suggest involving them, obviously as an external spectator, in specific meetings of a technical nature in the case of problems that impact production.

It will be used to start getting your own idea of how to best manage the manufacturing site's budgets.

To my surprise, I verified that even colleagues with theoretical economic training can become passionate about technical aspects and find further enthusiasm in them.

In a couple of cases, people were even involved in more technical activities, such as the management of projects for the construction of new PET manufacturing sites.

For me it is a demonstration of how the PET microcosm, a melting pot in which multiple disciplines are combined, is a real opportunity for professional and human growth, a catalyst in which everyone can truly realize their inclinations.

Manager

A manager does not necessarily have to be a good technician but must know the operational processes and systems of the manufacturing site.

For them the theoretical training will be similar to that of the technicians, although obviously their previous knowledge will make their analyses probably more in-depth.

In the case of manufacturing sites that are part of national or international networks, I consider very useful the possibility of programming alignments with the 'Corporate' references, immediately giving the new employee the broadest possible perspective. For the 'practical' part, I believe it is essential to attend some production cycles.

Note on those managers. How long does an operational manager, that is connected to production, last in a PET manufacturing site?

It is a difficult question, in my personal experience at most a decade or so.

Production takes place at night, but generally the responsible figures operate during the day. If a decision-making chain is not set up that also involves the technicians, the manager will find themselves being woken up frequently during the night.

At the beginning, the reaction is dynamic and almost goliardic, but in the long run it gives way.

It is actually difficult to combine personal activities, especially family commitments, with a working reality in which, in fact, one is always available.

To give an example of how much this work can permeate the daily routine, just think that even today, after about seven years that I am no longer available to follow the nocturnal PET production activities, it amazes me to be able to turn off my mobile phone in the evening before falling asleep.

To minimize the impact, it is suggested to define a detailed list of actions related to the different events/problems that may arise during the night.

In the case of rescheduling of productions, it is better to define general plans in advance with the commercial service.

Working on staff training is essential so that it is self-sufficient at least for the aspects of reprogramming the batches and the reorganization of transport during the night.

This significantly limits the reasons why the manager can be contacted at unconventional times.

At the beginning of my work experience, in a larger radiopharmaceutical department (both in terms of space and organization and staff) than the PET manufacturing site, I remember that the then head of the shipping department Alberto (the roles were those of the most famous Italian car manufacturer, at the time involved in the production of radiopharmaceuticals), in the long evenings that accompanied the production of the Mo99/Tc99m generators, showed me his model of manager, listing the characteristics I had to possess to manage that type of production.

According to Alberto, like a priest, I should have touched many hands but without really shaking any. But I had to touch them all, even those which, by direct or indirect knowledge, I would have gladly failed to touch.

As a priest I had to develop the ability to 'listen'.

I think that in proposing this comparison Alberto was thinking more simply of a role of confessor/friend, a role that, however, with some rare exceptions, I do not think I have ever held.

Consultant

Based on my experience, highly specialized figures, such as the Qualified Expert for radiation protection or qualification/engineering activities, are often delegated to consultants. They may require the need to be incorporated into the company staff in the event that the size of the manufacturing site increases, including, for example, more production departments, or in the case of a centralized 'Corporate' structure with several satellite plants.

The motivation for choosing the consultant is above all of an economic nature: the production volumes should be able to support the impact of a high level of professionalism, which could hardly be used for tasks other than those for which it was hired.

Consultants are an extremely valuable resource, but they are in direct proportion to the sharing of their work with the company team.

If the consultant's activity remains unrelated, or is limited to providing information for a specific problem, two situations may arise:

(a) The information provided will be extraneous, or in the most fortunate cases difficult to insert, in the context of the manufacturing site.
(b) The business team will get used to considering the issue addressed by the consultant as detached from routine, effectively creating an impoverishment of knowledge and forcing the company to have a continuous link with the consultant.

My suggestion is to identify in the company team, preferably an operational member of the PET manufacturing site, a reference figure, different from the top figures.

This should not be difficult, given that in recent years the level of average education has risen with an increase in the number of graduates.

The identified figure will not replace the consultant, and some skills both in terms of qualifications and knowledge cannot be improvised, but to develop a specific sensitivity within the team. In my experience, rather than having a ready answer to all questions, it is essential to have the sensitivity to the fact that a specific problem exists and that a specific situation must be analysed from multiple points of view.

As an example, I mention the possibility that the product can be shipped from Italy or to any EU country in countries outside the European Community.

In addition to the perhaps more 'natural' aspects for the PET manufacturing site, I am thinking, for example, of product specifications, release, and regulatory authorizations, and it is essential that the staff involve in the discussion a component that delves into financial, tax, and customs aspects.

A multidisciplinary team that requires univocal coordination by the manufacturing site, even if the issues addressed are very far from the strictly pharmaceutical ones.

An example of advice used effectively is that inherent in the initial phase of the construction of a radiopharmacy or PET manufacturing site.

Here the external support can be varied: engineering, qualification, and validation of equipment and systems or the implementation of the entire quality system.

The risk, more than perhaps in the consultancy required on a site that is already operational, is that the information provided, often extreme or very conservative, is not examined both for actual needs and for sustainability.

Sustainability in a broad sense: economic because an oversized plant requires management costs (we think of maintenance) higher than the possibility of return on investment and human resources that will have to manage the system in the years to come.

Chapter 2
Engineering Solutions (from a Non-engineer) and Equipment

Abstract The author provides some 'engineering' operating suggestions applicable during the construction of a new radiopharmaceutical manufacturing site or a refurbishment project.

Keywords Redundancy · Ease of access · Traceability · Knowledge of the system · Spare parts · Family lexicon

Few advice that I take the freedom of suggesting in this sector.

The strongest, dictated more by my operational experience, is based on two concepts: simplicity and ease of access to systems and equipment.

We must consider that, in addition to the problems of a pharmaceutical nature, the PET implant must also meet the radiation protection standards.

Simplicity because the temptation is that, when faced with the proposed solutions, we have an attitude very similar to what the most 'technological' of us have when entering a mobile shop.

No matter the often-limited level of use we make of it, our choice will go towards the most expensive possibilities and towards more performing devices.

The psychological mechanism why this happens is not clear to me, but I am instead sure that the long-term effects of a choice of this type at the plant/structural level can be a big headache.

The first rule is 'do well enough'.

Redundancy

Often the question that arises is: what happens if the system does not work?

The temptation to add a second back-up to the main (control) system is always very strong. But having two control systems means two systems to qualify and maintain.

To work in back-up of the other, a perfect match in qualification results and measurements is required. I remember long-standing discussions in front of a double control panel, electronic and manual (anemometers) for measuring the depressions of the premises. The second should have allowed reading in case of failure of the first. But the sensitivity of the two systems was different, so the overlap of the results was not certain.

The main question that must be asked in this situation is: why do I have to have two systems and if one of them stops working, would it actually be possible to continue producing? And doubts about the real functioning would affect the possibility of using the back-up system or not?

Let us imagine the simplest case, the one that guided the choice indicated above, of having two monitoring systems, one electronic and the other analog. In the event of a power failure, the electronic system would not have worked, and, in theory, the analogue system would have allowed production to continue. But in the event of a power failure, as the probable cause of the digital system failure, how many other systems would have been affected? I am thinking of production and QC equipment for example. Would it actually have been possible to continue production?

The production of radiopharmaceuticals is characterized by a very fast timing, everything takes place online. An anomaly like the one described above, even if for a short time, requires a risk analysis that is hardly compatible with production times.

So, perhaps, redundancy is not the element we need but the optimization of the primary system. For example, in this specific case, focus on the possibility of connecting the main electrical system to a back-up power system, an eventuality that, for example, many hospitals have.

Ease of Access

This is the most frequently encountered issue. All critical points must be accessible, but in reality, they are often not. Raise your hand if you are not faced with the need for maintenance in an impossible environment in our sector.

The peculiarity of radiopharmaceutical production is that in fact, with rare exceptions, it cannot benefit from long stops (and here by long I mean more than three days), it requires maintenance in the hours before and after, but often also during production.

It would therefore be desirable that accessibility has equal dignity, in the design phase of the systems, at least equal to the same equipment that is installed.

In the case of modifications to the existing systems, where changes are often carried out on structures that are already limited in space and technical solutions, the task is even more difficult. But this analysis needs to be done. It expressly requires the presence of a maintenance technician and an expert technician (production and QC).

They are the only ones who can actually evaluate how much the proposed solutions collide with the reality of production. So, please, fewer ties over the course of the project team and a plenty of space for those who will then use and live together with the system.

Traceability

There are countless episodes in which I myself or my collaborators were faced with the question 'but where is the valve' or 'what is behind that panel'? The most obvious answer, let us take a plan of the project, is usually accompanied by a smile or a shrug.

The changes, during a project, are many and unfortunately not always recorded for various reasons of which the main one is obviously the rush to complete the work. This does not usually constitute a problem in the first years of the plant's life, but it becomes so when the staff turnover erases the historical memory.

Here, my suggestion, in addition to the banal 'maps must reflect reality in detail', is to create a timely photographic documentation, specifically entrusted to a single person.

Why do I say to 'a' person?

Because the people involved in the project are many and often not each involved in all aspects of the project itself (e.g., environmental monitoring, radiation protection, ventilation system, electrical, connections between different systems).

It is therefore better to avoid the dispersion of this precious information by assigning its collection and 'custody' to a single person or function.

Knowledge of the Systems, an Important Opportunity That Can Be Exploited During Their Construction

As I mentioned earlier, the projects for the construction of a PET manufacturing site are all characterized by the need to be completed quickly, in fact they are late even before they leave. This is because we are aware that subsequent validation and regulatory activities, pharmaceutical or otherwise, can be uncertain in terms of timing.

So, it is worthwhile, in a certain sense, even correctly, to 'run' on the only phase in which the timing can be guided by those who build the manufacturing site.

Running also means carrying out different activities in parallel, also involving different companies. In this context, the enormous opportunity to allow those who actually manage the plants in the production phase to have a daily and calm confrontation with those who are building it can be penalized.

My suggestion is to try to set the project timing in order to allow the employees of the manufacturing site to follow the implementation activities in detail.

It is not an easy thing, both for internal staff (often with a background other than engineering) and external (who do not like to have curious figures around), but the benefits will be there over time.

Replacement Parts

The list of spare parts, especially for critical equipment, is often also included in the qualification protocols of the same.

What we often do not worry about is:

(a) Identify which of them, obviously beyond the foreseen preventive maintenance plans, is subject to greater or lesser wear.
(b) Which ones it is preferable to have at home so that they can be replaced even without the intervention of the manufacturer (if possible, of course).
(c) The feasibility of point (b) is subject to training by the manufacturer. In some cases, 'ad hoc' training can be provided with very high costs.

However, it must be considered that an emergency maintenance intervention could take days, if not weeks, and the same spare parts may not be available in real time from the supplier.

The choice of which spare parts to keep on the site cannot always be subordinated only to the manufacturer's recommendations. The intensity of wear, in fact, is closely related to the type and frequency of production. An industrial type of plant for obvious reasons is more subject to wear, particularly in the case of cyclotron and production plants and, in parallel, has more need to repair damage in a very short time. The presence of any 'back-up' sites in the area and a procedure to activate them quickly can reduce the need for replacement parts at home.

However, this choice must consider the logistical, economic and commercial aspects related to the interruption of production.

In fact, a back-up site is rarely able to guarantee the same service with the same distribution costs.

In the event that the site does not have a 'history' of experiences on the equipment, in addition to the comparison with the manufacturer, I suggest an alignment with similar plants operating in the area to collect as much information as possible.

Spare Parts Network?

It is an effective and cheaper solution than stocking parts at each individual site. In the event that there is a network of PET production sites, it may be convenient to store them only in a single centre in a logistically advantageous position, able to quickly send the parts to the satellite production centres. In the case of PET sites that are not part of a network, I am thinking, for example, of hospitals, it could be advantageous to create collaboration networks in this sense.

For example, the possibility of distributing the type of parts among multiple sites, with appropriate shared and updated lists, so that everyone can benefit from them.

Obviously, the benefit risk analysis must consider the actual benefit, including financial, and it is obviously essential to evaluate the options offered by the supplier before implementing any solution.

However, it can remain a solution in the case of spare parts that are difficult to find.

Family Lexicon

The best anecdotes in a PET manufacturing site are those related to unplanned maintenance.

It is in fact on these occasions that the team spirit is revived more than ever and ideas, not always brilliant, develop and overlap.

Furthermore, since PET is a continuous production, the discussion often has excited tones; the times for actions are very limited and always marked by the needs of customers who are pressing for a quick restart.

I remember a couple of episodes.

In the first, the protagonist is Marco, a Neapolitan, on a mission to the North to train as a Qualified Person.

Marco, with the typical affability of his wonderful city, was my first work experience with a Neapolitan colleague.

Marco suffered from cold, the humid climate of Lake Maggiore, did not help.

At the time, with a colleague, I was domiciled in a marina on Lake Maggiore.

A place, in winter, truly desolate but with a beautiful view that satisfied the frequent walks.

I said that Marco suffered from cold.

In the evening, at dinner, often our guest, we lit the oven before he arrived in order to allow him to warm up by swinging, not without a certain risk, with the chair.

All this while the fog of the lake enveloped our fisherman's house.

Marco had a particular predilection for manual skills, which combined with Neapolitan genius, always put him in the front row in the case of technical problems.

One night when the dispensing system had begun to show problems with the jaws that grabbed the vials, our Marco wandered around the dark runners of the research centre where we were guests.

When asked by Alberto, who saw his shadow passing by from the control room of the cyclotron, about what he was looking for, he repeated in dialect 'I have to find something'. In a second passage Marco appeared with a small soldering iron, firmly in his hands.

Alberto used to the strangest things (just think that knowing his work, many sought him for impromptu confidences in the middle of the night), but he began to wonder why all this movement.

Meanwhile in production, Luca, as usual cursing through his protective suit, was trying to understand the reason for the poor grip of the jaws.

Marco, who appeared next to him, having identified the cause in a possible stripping of a screw, begins the complicated phase of welding.

Having completed the welding, which seemed to work, Marco and Luca congratulate themselves on the success of the intervention but, in a moment of silence, there is a hiss coming from the machine.

Strange, says Luca, I don't think I've ever heard this noise before, but where does it come from? And Marco in return, in Neapolitan, 'I know where he comes from ...'.

The welding had held up, but, during the operation, the heat had punctured a plastic tube in which the compressed air flowed for pneumatic handling.

I no longer remember if the production was completed, but the phrase 'I know where it comes from' certainly entered the manufacturing site's lexicon, and there was no lack of opportunity to repeat it.

This is to say that, beyond the humour of the situation, good ideas do not always lead to effective results in agitated moments.

The second example concerns the autoclave, in this specific case the most critical component of the entire production process. It always has a certain effect, naturally negative, when an object breaks. Even more so when the object is inserted in a complex system that relies on it to function.

The autoclave in question, small (yes and no it will have had a volume of three litres) worked in close contact with the rest of the system that, by means of a robot, positioned the vials, filled them by perforating the already sealed cap and arranged them in order before sterilization.

At the first signs of malfunction, the autoclave begins to open and close several times, losing synchrony, the 'dance', with the rest of the system.

After a while, the sterilization process begins to stop and the towel is thrown away. Action must be taken. But how?

Given the long supply times for a new autoclave, European assistance is contacted, which overturns us to a Ligurian technician who works with dental practices.

After a long negotiation, an intervention is scheduled for Saturday but in the meantime, having heard that a similar non-functioning dispenser is available in Emilia region, the always available Alberto, who for a company mission would also have gone to Sicily on foot, is sent to recover it.

Nothing to do, here the autoclave from Emilia is unusable, we have to wait for Saturday for the technician to arrive, which happens on time.

Obviously (life in PET sites is always difficult...), the broken autoclave is not part of the models he maintained, but the technician tries to repair it anyway.

A whole Saturday spent in that clean room and in the late afternoon something finally moves. Maybe it was a burnt electronic card, I don't remember, but I certainly remember the moment of joy in witnessing a complete cycle and realizing that we would produce on Monday.

The subsequent dinner in a restaurant in the Varese area, all together, remains one of the best memories of my working life.

Chapter 3
Market Analysis, Is It Really Convenient?

Abstract The author analyses how to organize a production plan aligned with commercial needs, profitable as a financial point of view, and how to spread the 'culture of the PET production' in all the business functions.

Keywords Market analysis · Location of a manufacturing site · Logistic challenges · Sell dose or activity

Evaluating the convenience or otherwise of a PET manufacturing site is not something that involves only the commercial functions, but it is a team effort that also includes, and above all, the 'technical' experts of the product.

The analysis must start from the product itself.

The comparison I often make to those who are fasting on radiopharmaceuticals is that of the ice cube: imagine having to sell ice cubes, without having a freezer. If you had to choose where to sell the cubes, who would you turn to?

Obviously to those who are less far from the place where you are producing them.

Knowing the quantity and size of ice cubes you can sell is obviously critical to your business. In my experience, however, this first step is not often explored sufficiently but considered too 'technical' for the experts.

The radiopharmaceutical, in order to be produced, needs to put at least four main phases online: (a) cyclotron; (b) production; (c) quality control (which often begins before phase b ends); (d) packaging.

Each phase has its own time; in the case of (a) there are machine setting variables that can increase and decrease the quantity of F18 produced.

But be careful, the principle is not always valid that by increasing the quantity of F18 produced you can always have more finished product.

The yield of the product (amount of activity in the product expressed as the percentage of starting activity) depends on the synthesis process of the molecule in question.

There are situations in which by increasing the amount of F18 produced the yield even decreases.

To date, industrial productions are often carried out with synthesis modules that use 'cassettes' that already contain all the reagents needed to complete the synthesis.

The module and cassette system are controlled by software.

The timing of the synthesis is therefore predictable and with it also the yield (even if it is necessary to estimate possible variations of the same).

Then we move on to the dispensation, which can take place with different systems, with different times.

Obviously, also the Quality Control (phase c) has its times, even if here the advantage is to be able to start the tests in the first vials produced and the possibility of being able to start the shipment of the radiopharmaceutical before the checks are completed (but definition of 'ad hoc' procedures that avoid the risk that, once it reaches its destination, the product can be used without the analyses being completed).

To complete the picture, it should be remembered that the 'expiry' of the PET radiopharmaceutical, beyond the rapidity of the decay of Fluorine 18 (about two hours), rarely exceeds 10/12 hours from production.

In short, as you can see, a series of activities, each with its own standard time (more or less I would like to say) that affects not only the production capacity but also the timing of the product's exit from the manufacturing site.

When I think of the modern generation 'plug & play' cassette synthesis modules, I cannot fail to remember the synthesis module I faced in my first experience with the PET world.

In 2001 I was involved in the construction of the first Italian PET manufacturing site, managing production with two synthesis modules, made up of a variety of valves and tubes, provided for the manual loading of all the reagents.

The verification phase of the module before production, refined over the years, could also take hours and was closely linked to the experience of the operators.

At the beginning it was a real disaster; somehow the delay in obtaining the authorizations of the manufacturing site from this point of view was of real help as it was possible to test the equipment and accumulate experience before the actual production.

I remember that an experienced SPECT production operator after the first month of working with these PET modules, including the dispenser, came up to me and asked me if my intention was really to start an industrial production.

The same operator, after a few years, had developed a condition of symbiosis with the modules such as to be able to judge their status only by the sound of the opening and closing of the different valves and by the crossing times of the fluids.

Comment that reminds me a little of the literary testimonies of authors who, on the battlefields, recognized the calibres of the bullets and indirectly the danger of the situation in which they found themselves only thanks to hearing.

All this must be understood by the commercial actors who analyse the market. Things get complicated if the new production is inserted in a reality in which other productions are already present. In this case it will be necessary to 'insert' the new production in the production line-up in order to both satisfy commercial needs and not impact on other productions. This often also has an impact on the work shift organization model. Another reason to always keep technicians close to you in your commercial analyses.

Where to ship?

The sales department has to do a lot of preparation here.

If possible, I do not recommend entrusting this activity to people who, overworked, do not have the time and opportunity to prepare.

The person who approaches the analysis must have had the opportunity to learn the type of production, at least in principle absorbing the characteristics of the product and its limits.

If this is not done, if the peculiarity of PET and the product is not absorbed, the resulting analysis will be completely wrong.

The working method takes the territory and needs as a reference.

Around the site, with a system of concentric circles whose radius varies according to the type of territory and the concentration of the tomographs, all the opportunities with the possible variables must be identified.

In the case of large territories, I suggest one or more "brain storming" sessions in which to note down every little detail.

The priority and the company efforts must be inversely proportional to the distance from the production site, within a maximum of four hours radius, with a route by road, from the site in question.

It seems trivial but it is not.

In parallel with the identification of a customer map, a financial profitability analysis must be carried out, thus comparing all the costs associated with production and transport (if not reimbursed by the customer) with the potential sales figures.

The analysis must also take into consideration the possibility that, in order to meet the logistical needs of customers, for example the time of delivery of the product, other productions must be anticipated or postponed and the inevitable change in work shifts.

Why can't the radius ideally exceed four hours? Because we sell ice cubes, let us never forget that.

The more the ice cube has to guarantee the cooling capacity of a drink that is physically distant, the bigger it has to be. But my machine for making cubes has a limited capacity, so to meet these needs I will have to allocate more production capacity to the distant drink than the drink that is outside the door of my manufacturing site.

The entire PET production can be financially defined as a fixed cost, even if the quantity of production can be 'calibrated'. This is because, with variations in the irradiation times of the cyclotron, the volumes of the precursor of F18 and the number of primary containers used, the rest of the costs basically remain unchanged whether a single cube or many are produced.

I talked about road transport because PET production, borrowing a terminology used for food products, is for me a 'zero km' production.

In my experience, PET supplies by air, through commercial or charter flights, are always a gamble, especially for the following reasons:

– Handling times at airports

- The possibility that in commercial flights the embarkation of the radioactive package may be "refused" by the flight captain
- Atmospheric variability and strikes
- The rigidity of timetables that prevents, if there are production or transport problems, from being able to reach the airport on schedule
- The inevitable dead times of the various sequences of a more articulated transport chain than the point-to-point shipment by road
- Costs, which especially in the case of charter flights, can easily be double or triple the total production costs
- The extremely long notice time (comparing to the transport by road) to cancel the shipment; in case of a production failure the flight likely must be paid partially or entirely
- The difficulty of being able to make the customer accept prices for the supply that take into account the impact of transport, especially if a similar product can be supplied by competitors operating in the area who can supply the product by road

Air freight can be considered in specific situations:

- Customer willing to accept both the costs and the risks associated with the supply.
- Need to 'enter' a territory, especially if the possibility of opening a new productive reality in the territory itself is being evaluated. In this case, the profitability analysis of air supplies must be integrated with the analysis of the new site, and the probable economic losses of the first phase offset with the benefits of the second.
- Reasons of need and urgency related to specific patients or commitments previously undertaken.

As far as road transport is concerned, in PET production, it is carried out with dedicated carriers for specific customers.

Nothing prevents, except of course the logistical aspects agreed with the customer themselves, from being able to combine shipments in the case of close customers (the so-called combined shipments).

The limitation of this solution lies in the possibility that, due to manufacturing problems, the product may be shipped late. In this case, the impact of the delay for 'combined' customers will be more substantial than if they had received the product point-to-point.

These are situations, those of logistical optimizations, which must always be chosen according to the production trend. I recommend avoiding, especially if the delivery times are very tight or if the production site has recently manifested production problems. The economic advantage of the combination would in fact risk being thwarted by the customer's inability to perform all the analyses.

Selling by Activity or by Dose?

An age-old problem, not easy to solve.

But is it really a problem? Perhaps it is just a matter of carrying out different analyses.

Sale by Dose

In summary, it is the manufacturer who defines in advance the activity of the dose and its calibration and, in the case of multiple doses, also the time interval of subsequent calibrations.

In this way, the manufacturer carries out a direct check on the quantities of radioactivity actually sold, and there is no possibility that the user can inject more patients than those actually planned.

In real life, however, these terms may be subject to changes, dictated by commercial needs but also by specific customer needs.

The most common method is to dramatically change the calibration of the first delivered dose.

For example, if the calibration of the first dose is, as is commonly the case to cover preparation times in Nuclear Medicine, thirty minutes from the expected delivery time, this calibration could be moved forward.

If it were brought to an hour by the customer and the same decided to scan an additional patient before the actual time, they would have an excess of available activity.

It is clear that these "concessions" must be given very sparingly to avoid that, in their entirety, they can affect the actual production capacity of the site.

In my experience, they are a weapon that can be proposed in the initial phase of the commercial development of a product or site, especially when competitors are active in the same territory.

Beware, however, that going back on the concessions made is extremely difficult.

The price of the doses could in theory be calibrated according to the distance of the customers, but in practice it remains almost unchanged. This discrepancy can have a heavy impact on the profitability of the production lot in the case of a group of customers that are not homogeneous in logistical terms.

The impact, on the other hand, will be less when the number of customers is logistically close to the production site.

Sale by Activity

The manufacturer in this case provides the customer with the possibility to order a certain amount of radioactivity at a certain calibration time.

The limits of this method are the following:

– The product value can be defined per unit of measurement, usually the MBq. The value of the MBq used by the customer is however, first difficulty, different depending on its calibration. To supply 1 MBq to a customer who is 4 hours away, we would have to consume about double the activity necessary to supply 1 MBq 2 hours away.

It is the logic of the ice cube, remember?

What value then to assign to the MBq?

The simplest solution is to assign the value to a unique calibration time, for example the production time, clearly shared with the customer. In this way, the same quantity ordered by customers will determine the value of the purchased good.

However, it is clear that preparatory work must be done, because those who are far from the production centre will have to bear a higher cost for the same dose than those who are in the vicinity of the centre itself.

– It is possible that the radiopharmaceutical has, in its specifications, limits of maximum total activity per patient or maximum volume injected. In this case, the control of these parameters is totally under the responsibility of the clinical centre, and no longer of the production site, which remains unaware of patient programming.

In my experience, the sale of the radiopharmaceutical per dose guarantees greater control of the activity sold, preventing 'dose abuse'. However, it is not always applicable, requiring de facto detailed knowledge in advance of the activities carried out at the hospital level and the relative timing.

One of the main problems that I have encountered in my experience is the inevitable tendency to "dilute" the calibration times, both for the sale by dose and by activity, since it is a parameter that can more easily be used - at the same price of sales - to guarantee a greater quantity of product available.

Chapter 4
Manufacturing Plan

Abstract The author describes how to approach and manage the preparation of an effectiveness manufacturing plan including all the key stakeholders, optimizing the manufacturing capacity and considering back-up plan. Different types of doses are analysed.

Keywords Manufacturing plan · Confirmation to customers · Back-up · Maximize production capacity · Different types of doses

The production plan of a PET tracer is not something static.

In the days preceding production, it changes continuously, even with the passing of hours, as customers communicate requests referring to lots whose availability (days and shipping times) has obviously been communicated to customers previously.

The plan is based on the weekly/monthly planning of the production batches established by the site, by definition extremely precise.

In fact, since these are radiopharmaceuticals, in which the process begins and ends without interruption within a few hours and as the deadline is extremely limited, the lots envisaged for each single day must be temporally allocated 'in series'.

To complicate matters, based on the orders received by product, the amount of activity and doses required for the batch itself can affect the total production time.

In the case, for example, of a limited number of requests, the production time of Fluorine 18 through the cyclotron can be reduced, thus allowing the cycle to be completed in less time than necessary if there were many orders of dose of radiotracer.

In the case of manufacturing sites authorized to manage multiple products, this means a time plan of activities that reaches a level of detail even in the order of minutes.

It is possible that in order to standardize the activities and staff shifts, the times are set independently of the orders, taking into consideration a 'reasoned' production capacity based on the average of the request history or that is already calibrated to the maximum levels.

The latter option, however, has the disadvantage of wearing out more, even if not required by real needs, the equipment (with consequent more frequent maintenance and related costs), and to create a higher quantity of radioactive waste, with consequent greater exposure of personnel.

Generally, the production plan is made official the afternoon of the day before production. Additions/cancellations of orders from hospitals are absolutely normal, being linked both to hospital activities—which obviously must consider the needs of patients, the organization of staff, the various planned activities—and the diagnostic instrumentation, potentially subject to breakdowns and sudden maintenance that render the supply of the radiopharmaceutical temporarily useless and lead to the cancellation of the supply request.

The production site normally plans the scheduled maintenance activities annually, informing the commercial services and the Customer Service well in advance of any production interruptions.

In the case of unscheduled maintenance activities at the production site, caused, for example, by unplanned maintenance, the information is communicated immediately and the impact on production planning and the possible need for back-up.

The latter is one of the most delicate moments in the life of a PET manufacturing site.

In fact, it is not always possible to predict exactly when and how the site will resume activities.

Technical problems may require the intervention of external companies or the equipment manufacturers themselves and the need to find spare parts.

In my personal experience, the maximum duration of the shutdown of a PET site that I managed directly was three weeks, which I remember well as the level of pressure by the commercial functions and customers on the site has reached a point of extreme criticality.

What to do in these situations?

The first thing is, for the production manager, to try to concentrate together with the technicians, internal and external, and to define an activity plan that includes a time interval for the solution of the problem, from the worst case to the best case.

After having communicated it to all the company functions involved, it is essential to schedule a series of appointments/teleconferences over the period that you have defined as necessary to solve the problem, in order to provide univocal information to all concerned. At the end of each meeting a detailed minute must be drawn up with clearly defined actions, responsibilities, and timing.

If possible, advise your interlocutors not to call.

Phone calls, especially if actions are taken after them, are capable of generating confusion as they could add unshared activities to the list already defined with the rest of the team, without the others having been duly informed.

It is better to always ask to send written notes, 'hooking' to the thread of the minutes and leaving all the other people in copy, in order to include further ideas or reflections outside the teleconferences already scheduled, in the main discussion channel.

What is the best approach for a manager who must authorize the restart of production? Being optimistic, ruthlessly objective, or even pessimistic?

I think it is better to adopt an objective attitude, not to be overly optimistic even when the situation seems to evolve in a positive way and, whatever the type of maintenance intervention is, to test the entire process before resuming regular production.

This last point may or may not include the need for a 'hot' production, therefore with the use of the radioisotope, depending on the equipment that required maintenance.

In the event that the problems have occurred to the cyclotron, the synthesis module, or the QC equipment, they use radiation detection measures I believe it is good practice to carry out a hot production; in other situations a cold simulation may be sufficient.

The test can give rise to business discussions, as it inevitably occupies the space that could be allocated to the restart of real production, delaying it.

My suggestion, which arises from many disappointments originating from 'safe' restarts that then turned into inglorious failures, is not to leave without having tested the system. Only in specific situations, in which the risk is agreed with the diagnostic centre following the extreme urgency of the supply and when there are no alternative back-up solutions, it is possible to think of not carrying out the test and going directly to the production phase.

I mentioned the spare parts earlier. These may in my experience constitute the real 'black beast'.

Having a minimum stock of spare parts is essential, but it is even more important that the technical staff be able to use them. It is an economically difficult choice, but in the long run it can bring benefits, if compared with the risk of 'loss of production'.

In the case of a network of sites, the availability of spare parts can be the prerogative of many, increasing both the frequency of their use (reducing the risk of keeping assets immobilized for a long time in stock) and expanding the benefits to a wider audience on production.

Production Planning and Confirmation to Customers

Having no terms of comparison, I cannot judge whether what is required in terms of flexibility in accepting orders for a radiopharmaceutical is really the worst case in the context of the various product categories. Of course, in our world, flexibility and patience need to be abundant.

Having to allocate requests for doses of radiopharmaceuticals on batches with limited maximum capacity, it is advisable that, as they arrive, they are analysed to understand the level of use of the batch and, if an 'alert' threshold is reached, take into consideration the possibility of diverting subsequent requests to other lots.

In my experience, in order to avoid repeated and continuous steps between the Customer Service and the production department, it can be useful, as well as obviously carry out specific training on the products, to provide the Customer Service with tools, such as excel sheets created 'ad hoc', to allow them to carry out general analyses on the degree of filling of the batch in real time. In addition to simplifying life in the production department, the risk of last-minute 'surprises' is reduced, with the consequent corollary of reprogramming and discussions.

It is advisable to indicate a level of alert on lots beyond which, before the Customer Service accepts a new order, it is discussed with the Production department.

This level must be periodically reviewed by the production department, and it could in fact decrease—for example, in the case of a recent increase in production problems - or rise in the case of process developments (for example, increased F18 production capacity or synthesis yield).

Here too the problem arises of widening the audience of knowledge of PET principles to professional figures, I am thinking of the Customer Service, normally recruited with little or no familiarity with radiopharmaceuticals. And even here my experience tells me that you can have unexpected surprises, in a positive way.

In the activities carried out in Europe, involving a network of subcontractors, I came across requests from production sites that were anomalous compared to those I was used to in the Italian panorama.

For example, in Central Europe, in the event that there are new customers, the PET production site requires a 'procedure' from those who manage contacts with customers that describes in great detail the methods of access and the paths to be able to actually reach the nuclear doctors in their department.

The request, in addition to satisfying safety aspects, has its own precise rationale in the optimization of deliveries.

Not infrequently, in fact, inside the hospitals or clinical centres, refurbishment is carried out or simply the internal paths can change: keeping the driver updated on the actual path can avoid unnecessary waste of time that can turn into doses lost when for production or logistical reasons the delivery of the radiopharmaceutical is already delayed.

Not to mention that the routes of goods, nuclear in this case, are separate from those dedicated to staff and visitors and may not have the same level of visibility in terms of signage.

The list of orders received, whether already 'filtered' or not from the Customer Service, is then analysed by a Planner. The Planner must necessarily be a dedicated figure in the case of multiple sites to be managed; in the case of a single production reality, the role is usually assigned to the Production Manager or to the figure identified as 'Site manager' (a role that often coincides with the Qualified Person).

The Planner is closely connected with the transport companies, which assign the drivers to the various destinations, informing them of the exact delivery times.

It is useful to define a standard arrival time at the production site, in my experience at least half an hour before the scheduled departure. In the case of bad weather forecasts, arrival times could also increase.

It is not an easy life for drivers who deliver radiopharmaceuticals, especially in the cold months. The production sites are small in reality, they hardly have waiting rooms, and the entrance to the site itself of external personnel is strictly monitored (we are talking about both nuclear and pharmaceutical sites) and only contemplated for reasons related to maintenance, audits, or activities strictly related to production processes. In my experience, waiting is therefore often outside the building.

I remember a driver who, to escape boredom and sleep, accompanied himself for the journey with a small dog, named Birillo. In this case, access to the production site was strictly forbidden to animals.

Birillo, understood the situation, was so intelligent that as soon as he saw the security personnel in the distance, he quickly hid under the seats of the vehicle to reappear next to his master as soon as he passed the entrance.

Variations Before and During Production

Few elements such as 'adding' a dose at the last minute have the power to raise the tension and create disagreements in the manufacturing site.

I remember, I had just joined the company, and in this case it was iodine 131 capsules, which the ladies of the Customer Service tried to use myself as a 'carrier' to try to convince the 'surly' foreman to accept the additions.

The results were very variable, to tell the truth, since the power of the additions was firmly in the hands of the 'old' employees, being able to adduce them to a whole series of impediments that my limited production experience then prevented me from judging.

Often the requests are dictated by real needs, but it is not rare the possibility that they are linked to the forgetfulness of customers.

In all cases, beyond the picturesque aspects mentioned above, it is clear that the changes, especially in the vicinity of production, complicate the working life not a little.

The good practice of a PET department, in fact, requires that the laboratories are prepared in the afternoon of the day before production so that those who come in at night can concentrate mainly on production.

I am thinking of the preparation of the shipment, the cleaning and sanitization of the shielded containers, and the warehouse checks on raw materials.

Any variation that forces the staff at night to deal with activities that could have been carried out during the day reduces the necessary concentration and, in fact, constitutes a waste of time, even thinking about entering and leaving classified environments and the relative change of clothes.

During overnight production, the possibility of additional orders from customers is almost nil, while the variable of the change in the production plan due to internal or external elements remains (partial or total production failures, back-up, see next paragraph). The reasons why the site is unable to satisfy all the requests envisaged in the Plan are normally related to a reduction in the estimated production capacity. It is usually linked to a lower performance of the cyclotron or to a low synthesis yield. Normally, the plant engineering or Quality Control aspects, in my experience, have a minor impact and can be expressed above all through a delay in shipment, with consequent decay of the product 'at home' before it is shipped, thus reducing the number of doses available.

Back-up Plans

Potential changes in the course of production are added to the variation of the production plan before production.

Currently, especially for the most common PET tracer, Fluorodeoxyglucose (F18), there are more industrial sites available.

It is therefore common practice to have mutual support between the same sites, the 'back-ups', even if they belong to different companies, in the event that one of the same has production problems during the night.

Easy to say but of considerable logistical complexity, considering that:

1. The modification of the plan takes place mainly at night.
2. It may be necessary to modify the production plan of the site that has become available, especially if the new requests for 'back-up' require an increase in the quantity of radiopharmaceutical to be produced.
3. It is necessary to implement a logistic organization within a few minutes that allows the effective delivery of the added doses of radiopharmaceutical, possibly respecting the timing originally requested by the customer to the site that had to resort to the 'back-up'.
4. Sites that agree to provide productive help may logistically be hundreds of kilometres away from the site requesting support. It is also possible that there is also the need to 'hijack', in a very short time, the couriers of the site requesting support, already present on the site or about to arrive, to another destination (with the consequent modification of their daily working plan, which is not always possible).
5. The available site must incorporate all the detailed information on new customers to be provided, who may not be known customers, such as the references to which to send the product injection certificate, the exact coordinates of the hospital department, and any differences on the specifications, especially in terms of radioactive concentration, compared to the product that is normally supplied by the company that requested support.

Changes to the production plan, for own supplies or for those requested in back-up, always require a quick notification to customers.

This means that the operational staff of the production site must be trained and in sufficient quantity to be able to carry out this fundamental activity independently.

This information allows both to be able to reprogram patients and, in cases of non-production and/or back-up, to avoid, for example, that the patient for whom the dose has been canceled or postponed reaches the diagnostic facility unnecessarily or on time wrong.

Training is particularly important as not only are contacts with the customer delegated to professionals who have no experience in this type of activity, but the contact is normally referred to information relating to a disservice, which by definition is not positively received.

How to Maximize Production Capacity

In this paragraph, rather than focusing on how to obtain a high synthesis yield, an activity strictly dependent on the type of product and process optimization, I will worry about how to organize a production program that allows to optimize and maximize production capacity. Maximizing does not only mean having the availability to allocate more doses, this is not always the same as reaching the goal. The first goal is to allocate the 'right doses at the right time', not 'as many doses as possible'.

It is a job that the production cannot do alone, but in concert with the sales and marketing team.

The distribution of the doses in the batches that follow one another in production must reflect the logic of reducing distribution times to a minimum. In summary, the doses for the most distant customers should be placed in the first batches produced, while for the closest customers the production should take place in the following batch(es).

All this in order to allow all customers, regardless of their geographical location, the ability to obtain doses as soon as possible and avoid unnecessary product decay (before shipping from the site or upon arrival at destination).

The expectations of customers should always find a point of agreement with the production, in the logic mentioned above.

The optimization also passes through the definition of a precise calibration of the product. In the case of product sales for the total 'activity' delivered, the calibration should not exceed thirty minutes from delivery. If the calibration exceeds this limit or other 'reasonable' limit defined in advance between the salesperson and the customer, the consequence will be that the requested activity will have an important weight in terms of 'consumption' of the maximum quantity produced in the batch, guaranteeing the company sales lower than what it could have obtained by reducing the calibration.

The same applies if the product is sold 'by dose', where a clear indication is required:

(a) of the activity injected for each patient,
(b) time elapsed between one injection and another.

Allow me to digress on how a PET drug is sold.

I remember in 2001, the first steps were taking place to build the first PET manufacturing site in Italy to be authorized from the local Health Authority, discussions with the then sales manager.

His position, after having described the production process, the limitations, and the decay/use times of the product, was this: 'to sell a PET product it cannot be the customer who asks how much and when the product will be delivered but it is the company to have to define it in advance and agree it with the customer'.

A simple rule, I can say almost always disregarded.

But managing a PET product in the same way as other radiotracers, labeled with isotopes with a longer half-life and with a longer expiration, impoverishes the available activity and, in the long term, has an important impact on the economical profitability of the production site.

This does not mean having an insensitive approach to customer requests and being 'rigid' on calibrations, but carefully monitoring what is supplied to customers, analysing and tracking the real impact on the production of each concession compared to standard values. Periodically, I suggest at least monthly, these data should be discussed in the company with the competent functions (Production, Marketing, Sales, and Customer Service).

This role should be assigned to a function that actually has the possibility of collecting all information, including above all economic information, and analysing it continuously.

If the finances of the site allow it, a figure of 'business analyst', even a junior but trained in PET dynamics, could be a huge driver for business growth (greater awareness of one's own limits) and economic growth (avoiding the repetition of commercially wrong choices).

At the beginning of this paragraph, I indicated that to talk about profitability I would not have considered the type of product, its summary yield, and acceptance specifications.

However, I would like to underline how even these apparently 'technical' aspects must be analysed before marketing with the competent functions.

Having a clear idea of the product allows us to calibrate our real commercial offer.

In addition, some product specifications, I am thinking, for example, of the radioactive concentration, the reference calibration, the expiry date, can strongly limit the availability of the product to a more or less vast geographical area.

These 'technical' limitations may result in having to program two batches of the same product, in series, on the same day, with the first batch destined for the most distant customers and the second for the closest customers. The impact on pre-existing production plans/personnel and production programs is inevitable.

You understand well that if these 'technical' aspects had not been analysed in advance between production and commercial functions, marketing would have been severely impacted.

PET Doses for Commercial Purposes, Clinical Studies, and Collaborations with Pharmaceutical Companies

Are all PET doses the same?

In my experience, no.

I am obviously not talking about the drug itself but about the way in which the company must calibrate communications and its expectations according to the type of dose requesting. From this point of view, commercial doses are the simplest to manage. Simple because when the manufacturer participates in a tender or has to send an offer for the doses, the availability of the same in terms of day, time, calibration, and price must be well-defined as well as well-defined are the communication and financial channels with the client.

Clearly, also in this case there may be elements of uncertainty, in addition to commercial competition, but they are linked to production variables such as the reduction or cancellation of the activities provided or the back-up (when applicable).

In the case of doses for clinical trials (ISS) managed by the company that holds the licence for the radiopharmaceutical, a new component is added, which is the Medical Management department.

The real availability of the radiopharmaceutical in the various territories is not always clear in this department.

In some cases, I even realized a certain astonishment that there were such severe temporal and quantitative limitations in the supply of the PET tracer.

This is an extremely delicate point as the company has every interest, being the ISS its own study, in attracting the clinical centre by offering solutions that favour the use of the tracer without impacting its routine activities.

The methods of selecting the clinical centre, in this case, do not follow the same logic as commercial supplies in which the impact of the distance from the production sites is evaluated in advance but is dictated by the skills and affinities of the centre itself with the purposes of the ISS.

For this reason, in my experience, as the logistical 'screening' typical of commercial doses weakens, the supply for these types of doses can also be very challenging.

The impact of these supplies is heavy regardless of the frequency of production and the use of the production batches.

In the event that ISS doses are drawn from frequently produced and widely used batches, the variable to be kept under control, in light of the fact that the logistic position of the clinical centre could be unfavourable and require a lot departing radioactivity, is the impact on commercial doses and on the commitments made by the company.

In the event that the frequency of production is low, we could more easily find ourselves in the condition that the days and times of supply are not those desired by the clinical centre. In both of the above cases, extensive mediation will be required.

Sometimes, in the case of outsourcing, for example, in the face of the need to produce 'ad hoc' batches, it may be useful to share the scientific purposes of the research with the production site in order to raise awareness.

ISS doses are also characterized by another aspect: unpredictability.

I believe that by their nature, clinical studies must be carried out with different times and methods from routine diagnostic investigations.

For this reason, the doses are requested with a frequency that often appears irregular.

It is therefore complex to make supply optimization plans both in the case of impact on batches produced for commercial doses and in the limit case of 'ad hoc' productions.

The fact remains that coexistence between ISS doses, in which the main purpose is not commercial/financial, and the classic commercial doses are not easy.

My suggestion here is to keep periodic communication channels open with the Medical Management, so that we can be informed in advance about the various studies and, as far as possible, analyse the operational/logistical aspects of the PET supply before the clinical centres are selected.

It is also important to include clauses within the ISS contracts that clearly specify the conditions of supply, up to the minimum limit of doses that can be ordered (especially if the site produces 'ad hoc' batches).

Since these are company costs, obviously nothing is due to the clinical centre, they must as far as possible be managed within the broader financial management of PET sites.

The doses provided in the context of collaborations with pharmaceutical companies that use the radiotracer for clinical studies on their products have a certain similarity with the ISS doses. Also, in this case, we are dealing with 'unpredictable' doses, but since we are dealing with supplies that are paid for by the customer, it is advisable that the dynamics for the supply and the financial conditions are clearly defined.

It is possible that the company staff who manage relationships with pharmaceutical companies do not have specific PET training.

Without prejudice to the specific skills and responsibilities, it is appropriate, I would say fundamental, that, like what happens with the Medical Management for ISS doses, there is constant and uncensored alignment with the world of production.

The needs of pharmaceutical companies can easily foresee very challenging logistic needs, taking into consideration new distribution territories. In this case, the intrinsic limits of PET production and the reduced shelf life of the product are more evident.

Faced with these new opportunities, which often also require regulatory and financial analyses, it is advisable that an in-depth study be made on the beneficial costs of the operation and that the pharmaceutical company be made aware of the necessary commitment and costs in detail to support. This precisely in light of the difficulty of subsequently predicting the actual flow of doses and to avoid that the efforts made in activating new distribution routes, and even in some cases of new production sites, allow to obtain the desired results.

How to Rationalize Production Capacity When 'Commercial', 'ISS', and 'Pharma' Doses Coexist in a Manufacturing Site?

How to rationalize the production capacity when 'commercial', 'ISS', and Pharma doses coexist in a site?

This is one of the most complex situations in managing the profitability of a production site, those in which the use of production capacity is subject to three different types of needs and responsibilities.

In the case of commercial doses, they may be requested by the customer following tenders or private offers in which the company has played a pivotal role in offering the customer its 'product'.

The offer or tender implies that the company, through the local team, has already described in detail to the customer, before it begins to order, the availability of the tracer and the timing for placing the order.

Normally, a quarterly production plan is proposed, indicating the days available for the production site(s).

The information transferred to the customer also specifies the timing and methods for placing the order, how many days before production it can be sent, and the time within which the order can be accepted.

It is possible that the Customer Service receives orders even after the deadline: if compatible with the production capacity and the possibility of organizing transport, they are normally inserted.

Pharma and ISS orders are often lacking, in my experience, by addressing an audience of clinical centres not directly informed by local Sales and Customer Services, the actual availability of the tracer, and the timing of the production sites. The way to place the order is normally well known, being the standard form defined and included in the agreement.

In the case of the ISS studies, organized by the same company that markets the radiotracer, much can be done to cover this possible gap, at least at the level of initial information and subsequent updating (e.g., sharing of quarterly production calendars and on changed production capacities).

In the case of Pharma orders, the risk of confusion is higher than in the case of ISS doses.

The main reason is that the main contact in the Pharma company is often made up of a central coordination team that communicates separately with its local contacts, even in different continents. This centralization makes it difficult for the company that produces the radiotracer to understand how much of the operational information already transmitted has actually been transferred to the various regions. Furthermore, the clinical centres involved by the Pharma are many, and it is impossible, often even for the Pharma itself, to have a clear vision of which of them will carry out an effective recruitment of patients.

Therefore, among the three types of doses, the only one that can actually be controlled more or less effectively is the commercial dose.

The ISS dose, which has complexities related to the clinical protocol and the selection of candidates for PET analysis, is instead more complex to predict unless the company creates a robust link between the internal clinical structure dedicated to the ISS, the PET Planner and/or the Customer Service.

As for the Pharma doses, without prejudice to the real difficulty, sometimes even of the Pharma's themselves, of knowing the recruitment capacity of clinical centres, a solution to overcome the lack of information is to define not only relationships with the Pharma central coordination team but also with their representatives in the different regions.

In this way, the radiotracer company will have the most up-to-date information.

In the case of markets with strong demand for commercial PET doses, the ISS and Pharma doses risk being penalized. In order to limit friction and tension with the clinical centres, it is desirable that, in the contractual stage, the possibility of confirming or not confirming the request for doses according to the production capacity on the requested day is considered.

A constant alignment between the Customer Service and the clinical centre, informed in real time on the availability of doses in the different production days, allows for an enormous reduction in the elements of tension.

Chapter 5
Third-Party or Direct Production: Advantages and Disadvantages

Abstract The author addresses direct production (with own sites) and production with third parties, emphasizing the positive and negative aspects for both with different operating management.

Keywords Facility choice · Staff organization · Operational activity · Staff monitoring and motivation · Coping with changes

In my work experience I have dealt with both the production of radiopharmaceuticals in owned plants and with its own staff (direct production) and the production carried out not with own plants but by third-party companies (production for third parties).

Third-party companies make their organization and plants available not only to produce their own molecules but also those of any client companies.

A company that intends to develop the commercialization of a radiopharmaceutical, whether it is a new molecule or a molecule already present in the literature, can be pushed to resort to outsourcing for the following reasons:

(a) Insufficient organizational and financial availability to be able to develop and manage its own production sites
(b) Expected sales volumes of the radiotracer deemed not sufficient to justify, at least initially, the investment for the opening of a production site
(c) Limited experience in the radiopharmaceutical sector
(d) The absence of its own production sites in the specific geographical area in which production is to be developed
(e) The need to enter the market as soon as possible, while the company develops a project to open its own production sites

The subcontractor can also be accompanied by the granting of the licence to the third company to market and distribute the tracer in a specific geographical area. This occurs especially when the client company, owner of the patent, in addition to not owning production sites in the specific area, does not have the logistic and commercial structure to be able to distribute the product.

It is a solution that I have seen implemented, for example, in specific non-EU countries, with limited markets, already the prerogative of local companies with a strong commercial and distribution network in the area.

It is also possible to delegate your licence to third-party companies in areas of a country, or part of it, where the client company already owns production sites.

The choice in this case may be due to the specific need of the subcontractor, who does not intend to lose the role of reference in the territory or to the opportunity recognized by the client to exploit the availability and knowledge of the subcontractor's territory without entering into competition with it.

Direct Production: Advantages

(a) Production capacity and staff organization always aligned with the corporate commercial strategy: it is produced in the times and in the ways that the company requires.
(b) Ability to rapidly develop new productions or improvements of the existing productions using internal and external resources.
(c) Costs and turnover allocated solely to a company.
(d) Direct control of any production problems and related investigations, with a consequent reduction in customer response times.
(e) The absence of possible ambiguity in product responsibilities, managed in all aspects of production and distribution by a single company.

Direct Production: Disadvantages

(a) Significant initial investment, including plant/equipment and a dedicated and diversified team in skills, with experience in the field of radiopharmaceuticals. In addition to the depreciation costs of the equipment, to be considered also those of routine management (maintenance of critical equipment and raw materials) that will be added in the operational phase.
(b) Industrial risk borne by only one company.
(c) Need to continuously develop new opportunities to compensate for personnel costs and investments required by maintaining the existing production.

Outsourcing: Advantages

(a) Possibility of committing to a single product and for well-defined volumes, economic risk limited only to the commitments defined in the contractual phase
(b) Greater control of production costs

(c) Possibility to test the commercial 'validity' of a product before evaluating a production on a larger scale
(d) Possibility to grow together and develop future partnerships, regardless of the product covered by the contract

Regarding point (d) above I happened to face at least a couple of situations in which the subcontractor was absolutely ignorant from radiopharmaceutical production.

It was therefore necessary not only to build the plants and the same buildings in which to contain them almost from scratch, but to create the 'culture' of the product by also forming what would become the top human functions of radiopharmaceutical production within proprietary plants of the client partner.

It is clear that in this way the collaboration goes far beyond simple contractual formulas but turns into a 'path' made together that can foster and develop further forms of collaboration.

Outsourcing: Disadvantages

(a) Commitment of the third company limited to specific contractual agreements. If in the course of the collaboration different needs are highlighted, they must be discussed and negotiated. The terms of the new agreements, for times, methods and costs, may not be aligned with the expectations of the client company.
(b) Change of strategy or commercial interest of the subcontractor, possibility that the contract will not be extended or even questioned during its duration.
(c) Non-sharing of priorities, reaction times to production, logistic, or quality problems not in line with the expectations of the client or customers.

Direct Production

The Right Facility

In my experience, the decision of the production site is not always a targeted choice and perfectly corresponding to the best possible solution.

Often it arises from impromptu opportunities, from an expression of interest that emerged during commercial contacts or conferences, proposed directly by the hospital or by the company that wants to diversify its portfolio by proposing itself as a radiopharmaceutical manufacturer, for the first time or as a third-party activity in the event that production is already consolidated in it.

The opportunities are normally detected by the commercial functions that in turn verify the feasibility and possible timing of the project with the company technical functions.

Only in rare cases is it possible to build a system starting from a 'green field' and from a strategic/logistic choice defined in advance.

In the majority of cases it is a question of adapting existing structures, used for other purposes or that have available spaces or already existing plants, but which require updating/adaptation, in order to allow a production that meets GMP and radiation protection needs. For example, when it is necessary to 'bring up to standard' a hospital pharmacy that wants to adapt to GMP standards in order to manage a production (and perhaps market it) like a private pharmaceutical company.

In the event that you start from a 'green field' you have the opportunity to choose not only the location of the site, which is essential if you consider that we are talking about products with an expiration of a few hours, but also the spaces that you intend to allocate internally to the structure for individual activities (production, QC, shipping).

The risk is that everything is calibrated on the basis of the needs that can be glimpsed in the short term, that the right choices are not made (I am thinking of the spaces of the individual departments), or that the spaces that 'could' be needed in the event where there is a development of production or technology.

Obviously, it is always difficult to include all possible future needs in the initial investment, but it is reasonable to at least consider the possibility that there are spaces, even not used, which may be useful later as well as an oversizing of the systems.

What is often overlooked is that the changes made later are extremely complicated to make, for two reasons.

The first is that structural interventions on the building or plant almost always involve the stoppage of production for even long times, we are talking about weeks or months.

This constitutes a strong brake on the innovation of the site.

The production, in part, is based on the results of public tenders in which the company formally commits itself to the daily or weekly supply of the product.

Even if it is possible to find a back-up supply, beyond the costs, it must be formally agreed in advance with the customers, since the back-up product may have specifications even slightly different from that provided by the company.

It is also important to verify that the supply conditions in case of back-up may also be equivalent in terms of delivery and calibration of the product and that there is effectively complete coverage for the entire range of customers, obviously also non-public.

A continuous supply of back-up could foster a sort of 'familiarity' between the customer and the company, normally a competitor, of back-up, thus jeopardizing subsequent supplies at the end of the plant shutdown period.

The second, on the other hand, is linked to the approval of licences, both nuclear and pharmaceutical, which can also heavily affect the restart of production.

It is therefore important to define a 'business case', when creating a new production reality that, obviously within the limits of the possible, can compare the project costs with the long-term risks/benefits in not considering more spaces immediately or an oversizing of the system.

As regards how much space to provide the various departments for personal experience, both production and quality control are the most penalized.

Especially in production it is advisable that there is an adequate technical space allocated behind the production cells: a space that allows access to electronic and mechanical components without having to break the class of the production room.

These are solutions that must always be prepared during the design phase of the laboratories, and with the collaboration of future users, I will never stop repeating it.

The positioning of the departments must be aligned with the process to be followed.

We must always imagine that the operational team is entrusted during production only to a few units of technicians, often in connection with each other via intercom or telephone.

The more we reduce the paths, the more we will facilitate their contacts and their activities. To example if the cyclotron is located in a different floor from the production and if the shipping room is in turn in another wing of the building, it is clear that the workflow will be more complicated, especially if unexpected events occur during the production, unfortunately frequent in radiopharmaceuticals, which oblige people to interrupt their activities and to carry out maintenance support interventions or to support colleagues.

The geographical position and ease of access to motorways or airports are also fundamental. Even if the initial customer portfolio does not foresee the need for distribution by air, I suggest to verify, also through companies specialized in logistics, what can and what cannot be done from the site using normal commercial air routes, considering possible future requests.

I am speaking specifically of commercial air routes as they are the only ones, as already mentioned above, which can, given the limited prices, guarantee the economic sustainability of the air route perspective.

The use of charters, in fact, involves extremely large expenses, not always offset by the turnover of the doses shipped (obviously, it will depend on the type of radiopharmaceutical).

External Collaborations

Is it possible to have all the functions necessary for its development when starting a project? Some companies, especially multinationals, have dedicated 'technology transfer' teams, with experts in the field of validations, quality, production and controls.

However, this solution is not always available. I am thinking above all of small 'stand alone' realities, without previous experience of radiopharmaceuticals or hospital radiopharmacies.

The planning table obviously cannot fail to consider, in addition to the technical figures, the regulatory experts (relations with the local health authorities for specific licences and Corporate representatives, when applicable) and radiation protection.

As regards the qualification activities of plants, equipment and process but also for the regulatory part and the creation of a quality system, where this is not already present on the site, there are specialized companies able to offer a complete package of services.

The limit of this solution, which I had the opportunity to experience directly in a project in which the company had few internal resources to allocate, is the risk of creating—without an adequate 'filter'—pharaonic plans, certainly proposed by people of very high competence (often coming from the pharmaceutical world) aligned with the most advanced GMP needs, but difficult to sustain in terms of time and resources when the plant enters production.

Let me give a trivial example, which I have witnessed, relating to the microbiological control of environments that included Petri dishes and aerial sampling for a production area of less than twenty square metres.

The number of daily, weekly and monthly analyses (hundreds, many hours of work for the dedicated staff) was certainly able to comply with the most stringent requirements of the legislation but was clearly oversized compared to the real risks of environmental contamination, which we know, in the case of radiopharmaceuticals, involve very few people, develop in strictly confined environments (cells), also for radioprotection reasons, and use almost exclusively disposable materials (reagents and kits).

The problem is that, when the oversizing is carried out (perfect and repetitive periodic data) and the impact on personnel and costs is understood, a possible modification of the procedure requires not only long times, necessary to demonstrate that it is been verified in a suitable time interval (one year?), but this variation must be fully approved internally and may also require, on the basis of the entity, communications and approvals with national regulatory bodies.

It would therefore be advisable, during the project phase, that there is always a critical counterpart or at least that the consultants are made aware, as well as about the nature of the product, also of the real availability of personnel and financial resources that the company will have for the operation of the plant itself.

Believe me, it is better to waste time on these clarifications before starting the project than to accept, in the name of 'hurry up and avoid risks', any type of solution.

However, it is not unusual for the above discussion to also occur within the same company, for example for multinationals, in which the consultant is replaced by the 'technology transfer' group.

Allow me to say that in this case the discussion could be even more complicated, having at the base not the technical and financial negotiation with an external consultancy company, which in the end proposes a service for which the final responsibility is above all in the hands of the client, but the quality policy and the protection of the 'brand' of the company that decides the investment.

Especially in the case of companies operating in the sector of long-life isotope radiopharmaceuticals or in the 'classic' pharmaceutical sector, entering into the logic of PET production requires study and a lot of mediation.

I have already talked about the role of the consultant and how to make all the site employees actively participate in the project in the chapter 'Personal attitudes to approach the production of radiopharmaceuticals'.

Staff Selection and Organization

Is it possible to include in the company all the necessary figures for the development of the manufacturing site already in the initial stages of the project?

Unfortunately not always and the reason is above all economic. For a project for a new site, let us not talk about the 'green field', and we can even reach a period of two years before starting production.

However, I believe that the experience gained in this phase has an enormous value for the company that will certainly allow it to face the next phase, that of production and further possible development, with more serenity, constituting in fact a valid depreciation for the initial investment.

It therefore appears clear that the company must include in the project phase at least one person already experienced in radiopharmaceuticals, who can constitute an authoritative comparison with the many counterparts and at the same time 'filter' the various requests.

If this figure is not available, the possibility of having 'junior' people carry out periods of coaching in production sites that have already started can be extremely useful. It is appropriate that, in addition to the Site Manager/Qualified Person (the two figures often coincide), the Heads of Production, Quality Control and Quality Assurance are present from the start of the project.

Especially in the presence of a very robust and qualified consultancy service, it might be tempting to match the figure of the Qualified Person with Quality Assurance.

But please take in account that the inspection bodies could, in their analysis of the site, not limit themselves to verifying that an adequate quality system is actually present, but that it can be 'sustainable', based on the resources allocated by the company.

It is therefore very difficult, in my specific experience this solution was rejected, that a single person can combine the two responsibilities together.

This reflection obviously does not only concern Quality Assurance but all other departments.

Where to recruit the employees of a PET manufacturing site?

The world of radiopharmaceuticals is very small, and it is not uncommon for figures belonging to different companies to learn to know each other and very often to appreciate each other even in the course of their routine activities, despite being formally in commercial competition with each other.

I am thinking, for example, of 'back-up' supplies, which constitute, let me say, a beautiful example of mutual support, and which could also be interesting to develop in the sense of technical support without compromising the necessary commercial competition.

Those who think they can operate in absolute autonomy in the PET world unfortunately sins of presumption.

As I usually say, in PET 'the wheel turns for all' and sooner or later the moment comes when the implant, despite all the precautions taken, stops.

Word of mouth is one of the most used tools to attract and recruit staff.

It is also useful to include expert figures from the pharmaceutical world with no experience in radiopharmaceuticals. Maybe not in the first place, in the case of a new site project, but it is certainly an option to consider for an already operational site.

The person coming from the classic pharmaceutical will help us question ourselves and propose improvements that a small company, often self-referenced, has never considered or excluded a priori.

However, those who accept the challenge of moving from 'big' to 'small' need time, much more than people who have matured in the radiopharmaceutical sector, to be able to absorb and make their own those limitations, for example of a radiation protection nature, which impact on the processes and mark the limits of what can and cannot be done.

I have had interesting results by hiring extremely young figures in the company such as undergraduates or apprentices. It is always necessary to think about having a pipeline of potential candidates, also to deal with sudden exits of the existing staff members.

Times

I have lost my memory of how many times I have defined a project schedule that in the end was not respected.

In our sector the main variables to the realization of a project are linked to the regulatory and radiation protection aspects, but they are not the only ones and perhaps they are not even the most 'insidious'.

The first risk in defining the timing is precisely linked to the participants in the project themselves who often, in light of the inevitable stringent company needs, tend to 'censor themselves' and to be more optimistic than conditions allow.

My suggestion here is not to be optimistic, because positive news can always happen, but to define a minimum and maximum interval for each scheduled activity and for the entire project.

Defining the timing of a project is an activity as important as the individual project activities themselves. It is the time when all the things to do must be identified and deeply analysed in 360 degrees from all functions.

And the functions already involved or those we plan to involve are not always the only ones that can give us this vision.

In the kickoff meeting (project start meeting in which the activities are analysed) everyone must be there, and everyone must attend the discussion of the entire project.

The junction points between the various activities, the 'hinges', are by definition weaker.

A trivial example, which really happened to me, is that of a project in which the new production plant was built within an existing structure but not owned by the company that was building the new manufacturing site.

Once the new system was built, it was a question of connecting it with the general electrical panel of the existing structure. At that point, general panic. No one had foreseen this phase. No one had informed the person in charge of the link facility, no one knew who should do it, and no one had thought of the system overload caused by the new facility.

Fortunately, the capacity of the switchboard was sufficient but the unexpected generated many delays, creating, this is perhaps the most delicate aspect, general discontent about the skills of the project team.

The relationship with external companies that supply equipment and systems is important for a project. The risk of superficial timing also involves suppliers.

Given the peculiarity of a radiopharmaceutical production plant, supplies are almost always highly 'customized' and are produced and calibrated to the specific needs of the site.

The definition of the characteristics of what the client requires, extremely punctual and documented, must also be accompanied by a realistic time schedule.

Variations during construction must then be considered, especially for posthumous afterthoughts, often the result of a lack of correct initial alignment on what you actually want (despite the mountains of paper produced) and which can have a very heavy impact.

It is useful for the supplier to be informed of the general framework of the project and its criticality for the company. Not infrequently the supplier, possibly after having signed a confidentiality agreement, is also informed of the commercial impacts of the project and the risks related to delays.

For the most critical equipment, having a continuous monitoring plan, through teleconferences or face-to-face meetings on the manufacturer's site, can be essential. Delays are not always the result of changes 'in progress' by the client.

It is not unusual, for example, that there is an unpredictable lack of supply for the supplier of critical components. I have often recognized 'self-censorship' by suppliers when these situations occur, with the attempt to hide them hoping for a quick solution and without properly informing the client of the risk.

This is a critical moment because there is a risk of compromising the relationship of trust.

A transparent flow of contacts and continuous communication between the two parties can prevent this situation from occurring.

I cite as an example the supply of an industrial autoclave, as big as our son's room, intended for a 'classic' pharmaceutical production (not radiopharmaceuticals).

The relationship between the supplier and the customer had been severely damaged precisely because of the lack of clarity on the delays in the time schedule on the part of the supplier. In short, no one understood what was happening anymore, also because of the difficulty in communicating in English.

Sent on the site to understand what was actually happening, through targeted meetings with the supplier, in which I specifically requested to be able to meet the production representatives and visit the departments, I realized that the excessive number of orders, also accompanied by company changes, was the cause of the delay.

A step backwards on both sides, the definition of a new time schedule and above all a tight schedule of visits to the site, even weekly, made it possible, even if delayed compared to the project start forecasts, to complete the construction of the autoclave.

Between Dream and Reality

Who has never happened to be involved in a project in which we find the person who 'knows' that one and that other is who ventilates the possibility of accelerating certain activities?

I am obviously talking about lawful situations, linked to personal relationships with companies in previous similar projects.

My advice is to avoid them with care and to proceed, especially in defining the timing, with direct contact with the various companies.

Often companies change roles as well as new ones are added: it is not at all obvious that the already known reference still carries out that specific activity and can actually help us for our purposes.

Better to ask for information through official channels and get the precise reference for our request, if we do not want to find ourselves, in the best case, having to explain our need to two different figures instead of one.

How to Prepare for the Start of Activities: Not Just Production

Normally, between sending the documentation to the authorities and commercial production, it is possible to wait up to a year. How to prepare?

I remember that in following my first project to build a manufacturing site, an expert consultant told me to rejoice in that moment, because with the start of production my life would certainly change for the worse.

At the time I did not understand the joke, for the project (in fact almost a 'green field'), I was giving all my energies to the end and I sincerely thought that with the start of production I could finally concentrate on a single activity without the pinwheel of 'variables' and people of the project. I was wrong, he was actually right!

Preparation does not only mean testing the production process but carrying out 'stress tests' on all the processes that drive the life of the manufacturing site.

At the end of the validation activities necessary to request the production authorization normally, in light of the short time that has elapsed and the fact that the attention has been paid more to the completion of the qualification documentation than to the process, the production site has not a complete knowledge of the method, of the real difficulties and above all of the production capacity.

It is therefore appropriate that a production 'development' plan be prepared that takes into account the actual commercial needs (company or customer in the case of outsourcing).

In agreement with the commercial service, therefore, it is necessary to define the maximum expected capacity and verify whether the desired is actually compatible with reality.

Normally, the possibilities for the site to optimize the process are inversely proportional to the number of productions carried out in the routine, which, given the already substantial operational commitment, reduce the possibility of dedicating time to optimization.

At least one batch of tests per week is desirable, always followed by an internal review of the data.

In the case of production for third parties, it is advisable that the data review be shared with the client, who has the experience on the product and is able to also share the 'best practices' of other third-party sites.

In the case of outsourcing, the site must amalgamate its organization with that of the client, starting from the management of orders and the production plan.

Normally, against a weekly plan of available batches, batch confirmation and production orders are communicated at least two days before production.

However, it is possible that doses are added, no later than the early afternoon of the day before production in order to be able to organize transport. In the case of air transport, these time limits may be more stringent.

During production, there may be changes to the plan due to delays in previous productions, low yields, or technical problems. The site must inform the customer (with a concise note) and the client.

The client is responsible for possibly reorganizing the doses after consulting the customer, based on the information received from the production site.

Before, during and after the technical batches, it would be advisable to test the communication processes between the two companies.

An initial briefing, with a written definition of the contacts and key figures, is necessary, together with a clear process flow on who/does/what.

Warehouse

During the qualification activities for a new production, the material required for production and quality controls is reduced to a minimum.

In view of the start of production, based on the estimated volumes, it is necessary to insert an adequate stock (with attached estimated reorder point).

I take the freedom of underlining this aspect because, in the initial phase, there may not have been any problems relating to the procurement of raw materials that, on the other hand, may arise in the case of a request for larger volumes.

Night Shift Simulation

Especially in the case of a new site or in the event that the process has criticalities that require the supervision of expert representatives of the Manufacturing site (or of the client company), it could be useful at some point to also carry out test productions during the night or in any case at the times in which production is really expected. This is in order to try to make the simulation as realistic as possible and evaluate the actual degree of understanding of the critical issues by the operating staff.

Monitoring and Motivation

Monitoring

Monitoring the production trend is not an 'internal affair' of the manufacturing site.

Due to the type of production, night work, the need to 'rush' to find solutions, there is a risk that the discussion will remain the prerogative of the technicians and that the rest of the company, which does not speak the same language, has an idea vague and indistinct of what is happening.

It is therefore necessary that, once the KPIs (key performance indicators), critical indicators that highlight the progress of the Manufacturing site, have been defined with the company management, they are kept updated and discussed with the company management and with all the ancillary functions to production at least on a regular monthly basis.

Examples of KPIs:

(a) Summary yield (correct and incorrect)
(b) Bombardment/synthesis/dispensing times (including transfers)
(c) Product volume available for shipment (with and without QC rate)
(d) The total activity available for shipment (with and without QC rate)
(e) Batch reliability (batches successfully produced as a percentage of the total requests)
(f) Dose or activity reliability (the number of doses, or the total activity, produced with respect to the actual request)
(g) Production failures divided by macro-areas
(h) Doses/activities canceled (by the client or the site, with, if possible, evidence of the reasons)
(i) Doses/activities rescheduled (by the client or by the site)
(j) Tracking of shipments

(k) Operative margin per batch/period (month, quarter, year)

The KPIs from (a) to (g) are 'technical' data available to the site.

From (h) onwards, information processing is required, involving the Customer Service (h/i/j) and the commercial/financial service (k).

The distinction between batch reliability and dose reliability indices is very interesting.

In the event that the site has a production robustness of 100, i.e., all the batches produced successfully, and all the dose requests fulfilled, the two indices are perfectly identical.

$$\text{Batch reliability} = \text{Successfully produced batches} / \left(\begin{array}{l} \text{Failed batches} \\ + \text{Successfully produced batches} \end{array} \right).$$

$$\text{Dose reliability} = \text{Doses actually delivered} / \left(\text{Failed doses} + \text{Delivered doses} \right).$$

Below is a table (Table 5.1) that summarizes the advantages and disadvantages of the two different metrics.

In fact, we can define this connection between the two indices as per Table 5.2.

The 'dose reliability' approaches the 'batch reliability' if the number of doses produced for production batches is low.

A 'batch reliability' of 100% may not correspond to a 'dose reliability' of 100%.

A 'dose reliability' of 100% corresponds to a 'batch reliability' of 100%.

In summary, with dose reliability we can essentially measure the service provided to customers.

With batch reliability, on the other hand, the technical ability of the production site to comply with the production specifications of the various products is measured.

Table 5.1 Advantages and disadvantages of dose and batch reliability

	Dose reliability	Batch reliability
PRO	**Tracking the impact of failed doses on customers**	**Clear number!**
	For example, same batch, n.17 doses delivered and n.3 doses failed. Although the batch overall is successful, we have created a disservice for the customer	We know exactly how many batches have been failed and how many have been delivered
CONS	**Partial or fully failed batch?**	**We don't see the impact on customers…**
	For example, a batch with 10 doses failed over 20 produced could be considered failed? Cases may vary, depending on the overall number of doses	For example, if we consider delivered a batch of 20 doses, 17 delivered doses and 3 doses failed. What about the 3 doses failed? This is a disservice for the customer

Table 5.2 Connection between dose and batch reliability indices

Dose reliability versus batch reliability	Impact
Dose reliability LOW and batch reliability HIGH	Failed batches with HIGH number of doses
Dose reliability HIGH and batch reliability LOW	Failed batches with LOW number of doses

Obviously, there can be KPIs linked to the specific production or also to the transport needs (I am thinking, for example, of supplies by road/air that require close monitoring).

Particularly important is the analysis of production failures.

It is important that they are correctly classified into macro-areas, for example, synthesis or dispensing problems, in order to facilitate their monitoring and make any resurgence of problems more evident.

The analysis of the failure is not always immediate, it can often take weeks, especially when external suppliers are involved (for example, filters), and a unique solution is not always reached.

The documentary analysis must also be accompanied by an internal discussion, and we suggest a periodic comparison between the departments involved, Quality Assurance and maintenance in order to deeply analyse the events.

Motivation

It is always necessary to make the staff of a manufacturing site feel the proximity of the company.

The methods are different, depending on the role.

Site Manager

They must have structured time in order to remain connected with the top management functions.

By structured time I mean already predefined meetings, on a periodic basis, the actual development of which is traced by written memos to be shared with the management. It must be updated on commercial developments and all new initiatives.

It is the real trait d'union between the manufacturing site and those who work 'during the day'. If this bond is broken, it will be like leaving a lifeboat (the manufacturing site) alone in the sea.

They are the first to be motivated, both for the stress (let us not forget the H24 availability) and because the internal activities of the manufacturing site could become so 'engaging' for them to prevent from having that general vision, that perspective on where the company is going, which they and their collaborators (who, let us not forget, often work autonomously in night shifts) need.

Quality Control, Production, Quality Assurance/Regulatory Manager (When Internal to the Site and Not of 'Corporate')

These figures, with great technical experience, are generally not very aligned with the company's performance from the point of view of long-term projects and financial objectives. It is appropriate that the Site manager, like what happens between them and the top functions, in turn dedicates them structured time to periodically transfer the most up-to-date information.

Technicians and Operators

It is also appropriate for them, perhaps on a monthly basis, a group alignment with the Site Manager who illustrates the same KPIs discussed with the top management functions, but in this case trying to reconnect any downturns in the trend to the situations that the same operators have lived in the field managing the productions.

This is a very delicate point, as the discussion could be interpreted, if not well managed, as a sort of process.

In any case, expect that the operating staff can accuse you of all those situations (for example, shortages of personnel, inadequate equipment, alerts on critical situations not acknowledged) that for them are at the origin of the downturns.

Listen to them carefully and do not interrupt them.

In my experience, the fervor in explaining one's motivations, even if sometimes not always pleasant to listen to, is always an extremely positive element. As a manager you have to worry about silence and not about who 'gets hot' because they wants their work to make more money.

Coping with Changes

There always comes a time when, after having defined one or more standard processes, the site decides, for example, to reorganize the departments for new productions, change the organizational structure and, not infrequently, transfer ownership of the same to other companies.

It is not an easy time, especially for the operational staff.

Achieving a balance, made up of technical knowledge and scheduled work shifts that become a lifestyle, takes many months if not years.

The relationship with one's managers, in such small structures, becomes an integral part of the routine.

Changes in Productions

In the case of new productions, even the complete replacement of the previous ones, the first reaction, quite natural, is to repeat the same mechanisms already tested in the new processes.

If it is necessary to review staff schedules, let us expect discussions: from experience, after having standardized processes and maintained them for a long period, changing staff entry and exit times by even thirty minutes can be a point of friction.

It is necessary to explain to the staff what is happening. Avoid that everything falls from above, but make them participate in the fact that change is an essential thing for the company.

Stimulate their curiosity and collect their proposals. Furthermore, regardless of the changes, we never neglect the possibility that the hours of access to the site are also calibrated according to the quality of life of the employees.

One of the problems with PET is that it is the process that determines staff hours.

If the bombardment for the production of F18 starts at one in the morning, it could be legitimate, for example, to ask the staff for an entrance at midnight, to allow preparation activities. But an entry at midnight is equivalent to an exit around 8:30–9:00 in the morning. So, at best, the employee will be able to catch up on sleep between 10:00 and 18:00.

This means, in fact, eliminating or almost eliminating the possibility of participating in family activities during the week of shift (I think, for example, accompanying children to school or taking them back).

This type of situation weighs in the long run and is one of the reasons for the high staff turnover.

If in a situation like the previous one we had instead allowed the employee to enter, for example at 22:00, we would have allowed them a more natural shift. With an outing at 7:00, he might have had the opportunity to enjoy a family breakfast and accompany his children to school.

I am aware that these 'concessions' have an economic weight for the company and of the difficulty of organizing the work including ancillary activities to production in the periods preceding production (at night), but I am equally convinced that in the long run this far-sighted attitude can give in turn of returns.

Let us not forget that training a good radiopharmaceutical production technician takes at least two years, years in which the company invests time and money.

The risk/benefit in favouring human-sized schedules as much as possible must start from this consideration.

Change in the Organizational Structure

Organizational changes in a structure such as the PET one create impacts that are normally the more evident the more the change is 'close' to the operational staff, to the technicians who work in shifts.

I am thinking, for example of the figure of the Production Manager or of Quality Controls but also of the Qualified Person.

There is not always time to prepare a handover that considers the knowledge of the staff in addition to the technical side.

My suggestion is to never neglect this aspect and to inform the new manager of the characteristics of all the operators in advance.

It is also useful for the newcomer to meet the technicians in person and to compare themselves with the outgoing figure.

It is obviously possible that a technical figure, even a very experienced one, leaves the company. In this case, it is possible that there is a discouragement on the part of the staff, as there is also a lack of an operational pillar.

A solution to this situation is unlikely to be found, unless—which unfortunately happens rarely, not only in our sector—knowledge has been shared by creating back-up figures.

We therefore avoid leaving technical knowledge to the prerogative of a few or a single person, because for the most diverse reasons the person could leave us. And this, sooner or later, always happens.

Transfer of Ownership of the Company and Closure

It is not uncommon for a private PET facility to be involved in an acquisition by larger companies already operating in the sector or by companies that intend to develop their product portfolio by creating synergies with therapeutic drugs, for example.

In this case, the impact involves the entire company or business unit acquired.

These situations are characterized, by their nature of extreme confidentiality, by a remarkable speed.

Normally, there is no time to fully metabolize the news and the consequences. From my experience the first reaction is negative. People, accustomed to routine (not just the technical staff of the manufacturing site), risk losing their points of reference.

What will be of planned investments and new hires, for example?

It is therefore natural that there is a bit of bewilderment.

A delicate situation because PET production, in the meantime, does not stop, and all the critical issues present at the time of the 'news' remain to be resolved.

It is also true that in these situations there is not much to share, at least at the beginning, since normally only the top management of the company is informed of what is happening. In these situations, characterized at first by the circulation of the most imaginative news, it can be very useful for the manufacturing site manager to bring the whole team back to reality. For example, reiterating that the staff will be kept promptly informed, scheduling tight updating meetings, also retracing the success stages of the site, everything can be used to 'dissolve' the tensions and gradually assimilate the news.

The situation is obviously different in which the news is not the acquisition but the closure. In these cases, the routine operation of the manufacturing site becomes much more difficult to manage and guarantee.

In the only case in which I have been involved, however, we are talking about a traditional radiopharmaceutical plant, not PET, with a substantial number of people involved, the possibility of continuing with regular production is subject to many aspects (effective timing of closure, possibility of training and any relocation, the actual intention of the management to keep faith with the commitments undertaken with customers and willingness to make investments in this sense).

Chapter 6
Third-Party Sites

Abstract The author describes how to collaborate with a third-party manufacturing site, since the negotiation of the contract till the operational phase.

Keywords Third-party contract · Negotiation · Changes in the relationship

Does the Ideal Third Party Exist?

The ideal subcontractor has these characteristics:

(a) It is cheap.
(b) It has a professional and competent staff in the radiopharmaceutical sector.
(c) It is capable of producing our radiotracer without structural changes to the system that may require long times and high costs.
(d) It already possesses previous experience of national and international outsourcing collaborations.
(e) It has sufficient production capacity to meet the customer's requests.
(f) The production capacity is available on days/times actually compatible with the customer's needs.
(g) It provides for a production development plan in line with the customer's plans.
(h) It has a commercial strategy in the area compatible with the client.

It is very difficult for all the features listed above to be present simultaneously.

What are, in my experience, the most important points to consider when approaching a subcontractor?

There are three: staff (b), production capacity (f) and strategy (h).

Staff

A staff with consolidated experience in the sector guarantees a more fluid and rapid technology transfer phase.

A. Pecorale, *Essence of the PET Radiopharmaceutical Business*, SpringerBriefs in Business, https://doi.org/10.1007/978-3-030-97937-9_6

Furthermore, the expertise in the sector guarantees greater production robustness in the phase in which the product can be marketed, as well as greater attention to the quality policies required by the customer.

This last point is particularly important in the event that the client is one multinational that may not be satisfied with the specific needs of local regulatory authorities alone.

Production Capacity

Even if the logistics position of the subcontractor is perfect for our need, it could be limited by the actual ability to satisfy our requests.

Requests in PET are not only in absolute terms of batches per time period (week, month, or year), but must also be declined on the days and times available.

If availability does not meet our need, the site will be useless.

A shipping time that is too advanced in the morning or early afternoon may not align with the actual possibility of use, or severely limit it.

Strategy

It has to be verified the willingness of the subcontractor to remain within this role, without competing with the client.

It is possible that the subcontractor is a competitor of the client on their own products and is instead a subcontractor for the client on other products.

This position could even be an advantage for the client, who could benefit from the good reputation of the subcontractor in the area.

Even if obviously, it is not possible to think that the situations will remain unchanged over time, it is advisable that in the contract phase the effective strategy of the subcontractor and their willingness not to enter into conflict with the customer's plans should be verified.

If possible, insert in the supply contract an exclusivity formula if not for the specific product at least for the product class on the basis of the diagnostic or therapeutic indications.

It is very difficult for all the client's expectations to be fully satisfied.

The fact that the staff is junior is not necessarily a problem in perspective: the client company could act, with its skills, as a partner in terms of know-how, creating a synergy that can be consolidated over the years.

The major limit in this case is the project timing to implement the subcontracting, which will be longer than with an already adequately trained and experienced team.

The strategy of the two companies, even if not aligned, may not be an insurmountable problem.

Let us say the 'worst' case, the one in which the subcontractor is already a manufacturer and distributor of a 'competitor' drug to the one the customer requests to produce.

In this case, the customer, in the contract, must be very clear on the needs in terms of the number of productions, times, completion of release tests and additions/cancellations of productions and doses.

The same elements that I recommend to always specify with the difference that here the ambiguity can, in the routine, risk raising the doubt that the third company can use the slots, the production intervals, 'best' for their own product, with the risk of compromising relationships.

Unfortunately, I have direct experience of these situations.

Even anomalous peaks of increase in production failures, in a situation like the one described above, can give rise to speculations (often unfounded) on the loyalty of the company.

The point on which, on the other hand, we absolutely cannot risk it concerns the desired production capacity.

It is not always clear in the initial stages nor is it possible to provide precise guarantees.

If the subcontractor is available, the best solution for the client is not to make specific commitments on the programmed batches (in other words, they will be paid only in the case of actual dose requests) but to propose a series of possible days/times of production.

The latter may or may not be used.

Confirmation by the customer will take place well in advance, for example on the Friday of the week preceding production. In this way, the client will only compensate the subcontractor for the lots whose need was actually confirmed the previous week and which are then actually produced.

This solution is mostly applied in emerging production sites, with a limited utilization of the overall production capacity and with a lot of availability.

In the case of sites with already a consolidated portfolio of products this solution is not always accepted, indeed in my experience almost never.

The only solution here is to 'block' the slots in a calendar already predefined on a contractual level.

The Contract and Room for Manoeuvre

When I started dealing with contracts with third parties, the first reaction was to consider them as an activity of the exclusive prerogative of lawyers.

A field that, having no specific academic preparation, initially put me in difficulty.

From experience I have learned that, unless there are particular situations that require a specific legal or regulatory feasibility analysis (for example on the possibility that a public hospital can carry out subcontracting activities for private companies or for legal clarifications related to environmental aspects), it is better to start by first clearly defining the financial, production, logistical and quality terms, involving the appropriate figures on both sides, then leaving the lawyer with the task of amalgamating and expressing the different needs also in the appropriate language.

Activity that takes a long time at the first experience, but once the standard 'form' has been defined, it can be reproduced in other situations, modifying it only for the financial and productive part.

Negotiation with the Subcontractor

The need to organize a radiotracer production network in a specific country or a wider territory is highlighted.

Do you contact a possible subcontractor who has the sites that logistically can be aligned with our needs: how to manage the negotiation?

In my experience this is the time when rather than talking to the counterpart, it is necessary to internally clarify what we actually need.

We often approach the discussion without actually knowing what we want.

As I have already indicated, the definition of what are the actual needs of customers, which therefore allow the company to make a detailed forecast of the quantitative/temporal estimates of the doses needed in the individual territories, is a long job that requires resources and time structured.

Attention, this is not to say that even if in possession of non-detailed information, it is not useful to speak with the subcontractor. It is always important to align on commercial strategies and also to create a certain expectation for a new phase of collaboration.

But to negotiate a contract and especially the economic part of it, the following points must be kept in mind:

1. Logistic references of every single potential customer
2. In broad terms the needs for each of them (the number of doses per year, better if divided by quarter if not by single month)
3. Estimated dose selling price
4. The number of average doses needed for each single lot
5. The minimum shipment time to allow us to satisfy the greatest number of requests (bearing in mind that a postponed shipping time is equivalent to reducing the number of doses that the customer can actually use, as the activities of the diagnostic centres are limited in most cases until late afternoon).

The points indicated above allow the client to lay the foundations for a business case and to actually understand how many lots we need and how much we are willing to compensate the subcontractor.

The strategy, often dictated by haste, of starting a negotiation without having the above points clear and focusing only on the lowest price can lead to the following consequences:

1. Prove to be superficial, approximate and worse still give the impression of not being convinced of the quality of our offer. The subcontractor, let us never forget, knows the business as much as we do if not better than us, looking not only for an opportunity for economic growth but above all for an element of innovation, improvement of their brand and long-term sustainability of their business. A discussion that has no solid basis but is clearly aimed at saving or, worse still, trying to transfer the risk to one or the other, demeans our and their project.
2. The days and the temporal arrangement of the lots proposed by the subcontractor are what favour their business, not ours. Allocated lots are then proposed either

very early in the morning or the last possible lot of the day. In both cases, the optimization of doses is penalized. A batch produced early in the morning requires the product to stop and decay for hours at the production centre before it can be shipped to customers within a short distance. Shipping in the late morning or very early afternoon, on the other hand, limits delivery to long-distance customers and the actual use of the product.

3. A low economic proposal may entice the subcontractor to integrate the lot fee with a share in the profits from the sale of the doses or to request exclusivity on one or more territories. In my opinion, this method should always be avoided, especially in the case of new tracers in which the commercial forecast has greater elements of uncertainty than an already consolidated tracer in the market: we could therefore find ourselves having to discuss not only internally but also with the same subcontractor (who, for example, could be concerned about the risk that the client will reduce the sale price potentially defined in the negotiation phase, with a consequent reduction in its margin).

4. A great waste of time. Betting everything on the price means to excessively enrich the contractual conditions as a corollary on the productions. For example, the payment terms required will be minimal; in the event of production failure, it is presumable that you want to investigate the liability thoroughly (the customer is responsible for the robustness of the process); the subcontractor will try to widen the links of the withdrawal conditions (in the event that a more profitable tracer should emerge).

Where to Start to Negotiate the Price of a Production Batch?

Normally, a bit like it happens in all product categories, from the average of the prices you are aware of, obviously starting from your data.

For reasons of industrial secrecy, it is difficult to carry out a real 'market survey' involving other companies.

An average that will have to be weighted if extended territories are taken into consideration, where the cost of living is very different. I have already mentioned the strong differences between the costs of batches between Northern and Southern Europe, offset by a general increase in the price of doses.

An average cost value of the batch is compared with the average selling price of the tracer, for example per dose, and normally, an attempt is made to propose to the third-party site a starting value that allows to reach a positive margin even if a minimum number of doses. This, of course, is to try to minimize the potential risk that the initial sales hypotheses are not effectively reflected on the market.

Neither of the above two methods, in my experience, has led to effective results.

The reason is one, the real situation of the production site is hardly taken into consideration, which can be extremely different:

– The site already has a saturated production plan with many 'slots' occupied, perhaps with products already capable of guaranteeing high profitability.
– Any available slots are at times that do not allow full use of the tracer (production termination very early in the morning or too late in the day).
– The site already intends to develop new tracers, capable of guaranteeing high profitability.
– The site has already established multi-year committments with other customers on the various manufacturing slots, which cannot be changed.
– Need to make changes to the existing systems or to add shielded cells and/or new synthesis modules.
– The site does not have enough space or staff to be able to manage new productions. We cannot therefore think of convincing the site to replace the current tracers produced with ours, above all by offering prices at the minimum discount, unless:
  – our tracer does not have a strong 'novelty' character on the market. The introduction of the new tracer, even if not a source of greater profit, would satisfy the common and just tendency of the sites to want to propose themselves as excellence for new tracers on the local market.
  – The possibility of exponential growth in volumes. I am thinking of the situation in which the diagnostic radiotracer is aligned with research plans at an advanced stage for the development of therapeutic drugs with a similar biological target.
  – The client company considers (and expresses in clear terms at the contractual level), precisely in the light of a possible plan to increase volumes, the willingness to gradually increase the price of the lots and their number.

If the above conditions are not applicable, all that remains is to start the negotiation with full awareness of its limits.

My suggestion is to try to propose a progressive increase over the years of the client's commitment, in terms of batch value or number. This solution allows the client company to recover precious time to 'refine' its commercial strategy, benefiting in the initial period from a lower economic commitment.

How Detailed Does a Contract Need to Be?

The room for manoeuvre, on both sides, in the case of a generic contract will obviously be much greater. But, at least in PET, this is a double-edged sword.

It is never possible to be generic on production capacity and in the economic part for the reasons already indicated above.

Considering that the average duration of a contract is five years, renewable for another five, it is necessary to evaluate together what are those parameters that, in such a long time, could change and invalidate our initial assessments on which the contract itself was based. I am thinking, for example, of raw materials that in the case of PET can be subject to variations in costs due to the market.

In the event that the raw materials are supplied by the client, if it is a pure subcontracting contract, the option of providing them with a 'controlled' price that provides only a minimum margin for the client can be evaluated.

The cost incurred by the subcontractor for the purchase of raw materials from the customer is normally 'reimbursed' by the customer 'on top' of the value of the batch.

This part, in principle variable because it is linked to production costs, may possibly be subject to updating year by year.

This solution allows us to exclude this value from the negotiation on the actual production price of the lot, making it in some way 'transparent' in the subcontractor's budget.

Obviously, this choice must be carefully evaluated by the customer, for whom the raw materials will in fact be additional costs to the costs incurred for the production and distribution of the batch.

It is also useful to include a contract in the negotiation that considers the possibility that the subcontractor organizes the logistics of shipping the products.

I believe this last point is almost more important than the production part.

The possible variations of the production, from the low yield and the recalibration of the doses up to the cancellation of the same, cannot be foreseen if not in part (for example, the cancellations of the customer).

Entrusting the control of logistics to the customer will require the client company to have a continuous alignment with the production site, even at unconventional times.

Even if this were possible, the result will not always be satisfactory due above all to the inevitable delays in communication due to the rapidity of the events that characterize PET production.

The logistics contract must define the current product distribution territories and must be flexible enough to consider the possibility that territories can be added without the need to formally update it (I am thinking of e-mail communications rather than legal reviews and signature of the top management of companies).

My suggestion is to draw up a table of customers and transport costs that the parties will keep constantly updated.

It is preferable that there is no specific commitment by the client company to use only and exclusively the logistics service of the subcontractor.

It is possible, in fact, that some particular logistic solutions, I am thinking of air transport via charter, can be better managed by the client if, for example, the company is of international dimensions and there are already previous experiences and relationships/contracts with companies specialized in sector.

Normally, in the logistics contracts proposed by the subcontractor, the transport is fully reimbursed by the customer with the possible addition of a margin for the coordination service.

If the client believes that he can carry out these logistic activities internally, without the need for the support of the subcontractor, I suggest to carefully check the resources necessary and to evaluate the seriousness of the commitment in light of the absolute criticality of transport for the success of the PET business.

Another important element are the possible penalties, for partial or complete failure of production or for failure to supply the service in its entirety (I am thinking of the refusal to supply the customer with the production intervals defined in the contract).

The request for a penalty by the client, even if not raised when a contract is defined, will certainly be advanced by the company, of this rest assured, when the third-party site will have the first production difficulties.

My position on the question 'are penalties foreseen' is 'no'.

My answer to the next question 'why?' it is always the same: 'at least in PET they are perfectly useless'.

Why are they useless?

At least for four reasons:

(a) In the event of batch failure, the client does not pay the lot. The penalty for the subcontractor, therefore, is in fact already inherent in the lack of production itself. The subcontractor will have unnecessarily invested time, personnel and resources, without any benefit. It is difficult to think that the disservice may have been deliberately caused unless there is a lack of professionalism. In this case, however, it can and must be detected in the initial phase of 'technology transfer' and in the technical batches that precede the start of production.

(b) What penalty can I apply? A theoretically possible solution may be to charge for lost turnover. However, the amount of the penalty varies according to the doses produced. But in PET the doses produced vary lot by lot according to the needs of the market and commercial management, including the sale price, and it is the complete prerogative of the customer. I find it difficult for a subcontractor to accept such unmanageable and quantifiable risks. The consequence of insisting on this point is that the subcontractor guarantees themselves by raising the value of the lot to levels not sustainable by the client.

(c) It takes trust. I am not speaking only of 'intangible' aspects, linked to the willingness of companies to move towards a common strategy, but also of operational aspects.

The subcontractor must be enabled to dare and develop product knowledge in order to guarantee reliability and an ever-increasing production capacity.

The system of penalties, whatever it may be, creates the risk of demotivating and making the subcontractor too cautious in the face of production needs that hopefully ever increase.

(d) Responsibility could be shared between subcontractor and customer. Situation that can occur especially if it is a product developed by the customer, where the same has indicated the materials and reagents to be used.

In the production of radiopharmaceuticals, the production of the radioisotope, the active principle and the distribution of the finished product are happening in a very limited period of time.

There are many phases and, in the case of problems in the processes (also possible due to human causes), an unambiguous conclusion of the investigation is not always reached.

For this reason, the application of a penalty itself, in light of the long analysis times or the impossibility of finding a real cause of the problem, may simply not be applicable.

A separate case is the partial failure of the lot.

The batch is regularly produced, but the synthesis yield or problems occurring during dispensing or interruptions that lead to a decrease in available activity prevent all requests for scheduled doses from being met.

This is a situation that can be partially resolved trying to align the requests with the production trend, avoiding to allocate a number of doses that oblige the site to reach the maximum capacity, in order to always have a 'spare' in case of need.

Sometimes this is not possible, and production is carried out anyway, it is appropriate that the risk be shared and that the supplies to be given priority are clear.

Monitoring

Does the subcontractor need to be monitored? The answer is obviously yes.

On how to carry out the monitoring I distinguish two types: 'political' and production.

Political monitoring requires that the top figures of the two companies involved meet.

The frequency is usually directly proportional to the production volumes and to the commercial variables that arise, for example in the case of new territories that require a production or logistic reorganization or important customers to serve.

Production monitoring, on the other hand, is linked to the control of operational parameters and production robustness (reliability).

On this last point, the level of detail that you want to achieve in knowing what happens at the subcontractor is linked to various factors:

(a) Experience of the subcontractor in the production of radiopharmaceuticals
(b) Effective ability to control the production process, on both sides
(c) Need to collect data to support subsequent product optimizations
(d) The ability to monitor, through the customer's experience, any negative trends which, while not affecting current production, could generate, if not resolved, an increase in production failures

(A) In the event that the third-party site has limited or no experience in production, it is important that there is a constant presence on the part of the client company. In this case, a sort of continuous 'training' is configured, which begins in the technology transfer phase and continues in routine production, through the sharing of the most significant production data and the periodic presence of the customer's expert technical staff during the production.

(B) The processes transferred to the subcontractor are not always 'mature' and can guarantee sufficient reliability; for this reason it is worth setting up a process as in point (a).

(C) Third-party sites can also be used as a 'development laboratory' for subsequent process optimizations.

In these cases, an 'ad hoc' agreement is usually defined for a project in which the subcontractor estimates the resources, the necessary materials, the time slots in which to allocate the productions and of course the costs.

It is appropriate that:

(a) The purpose, timing and intellectual right of the results (which must also be shared with other third-party sites involved in similar projects) are included within a specific contract.

(b) Routine activities are strictly separated from project activities to avoid risky intersections.

(D) This is a point that mainly engages the client, who processes the amount of technical information received from subcontractors and overlaps and compares them with their experience and data from the entire network.

The operating methods with which information is transferred from the subcontractor to the client can benefit from innovative IT systems. For example, allowing all subcontractors to access an online platform of the client to enter the data, avoiding that they are sent separately, for example via e-mail to the client's contact person(s), will allow to optimize the resources dedicated to the insertion data and to focus only on statistical analysis. Periodically, the data must be shared with subcontractors.

Normally, the sharing, in person, via e-mail or through teleconferences, takes place with one subcontractor at a time.

Creating a shared network among everyone, also giving the subcontractors themselves the opportunity to communicate with each other, can be evaluated if there are no obvious conflicts of a commercial nature and if there is the guarantee that the client is always informed of the nature and the conclusions of the comparisons between the subcontractors. This is to avoid that, without their knowledge, actions can be implemented that could have an impact on supplies and, not least of course, on the quality of the product.

On the same track the possibility of allowing subcontractors to meet, get to know each other and visit their respective sites.

A mutual enrichment that, however, needs, I am aware of, a very 'far-sighted' approach on the part of the client.

Life as a Couple, Loves & Quarrels

As in a life as a couple, loves and quarrels characterize the journey of the client and the subcontractor together.

There will be loves if there is:

(a) Willingness to collaborate, common strategic vision, even beyond the production of radiopharmaceuticals
(b) Ability to reach and exceed challenging productive and economic objectives

There will be quarrels if:

(a) It is not possible to achieve the objectives, perhaps because the expectations of production capacity and market forecasts have been overestimated.
(b) The production becomes for the subcontractor a 'waste of time' an obstacle to other opportunities (for example, own products) developed in the meantime.

Let us analyse above all the second situation, since the possible solutions for the first have already been indicated in the previous chapter.

Almost always the change of position of the subcontractor can be anticipated if the client company dedicates structured time to analyse the operational and sales performance also from their point of view. Unfortunately, this is a point that is often underestimated.

The client company spends little time to get into the point of view of those who produce and usually does so when things, commercially and productively, go wrong.

An example from my personal experience: a lack of production problems and very high sales in the region covered by the subcontractor. An optimal situation that for me did not require specific investigations.

However, the subcontractor's vision was developing differently.

The economic basis, based on the remuneration of the batches only and the visibility on the increase in the doses required by the market from the client and the relative turnover, was giving the production site the certainty that there was a growing disparity between the benefits of the two companies.

This disparity emerged only when the client requested, precisely in light of the growing needs in the area, an increase in the number of production lots.

The negotiation, which then ended positively, was however 'poisoned' by a strong resentment on the part of the subcontractor precisely for the benefits one of the two partners had enjoyed in previous years.

Resentments that the client had not heard of for a lack of attention and in-depth analysis.

It is possible to quarrel not only for economic but also technical reasons, especially in the case of problems involving the product of which the customer has the intellectual property or in the raw materials supplied by the same.

The analysis of the causes of a problem, in pharmaceuticals and in PET in particular, takes time, and it is not always easy to understand whether it depends on the activities of the site or on the process and materials provided by the client.

In the case of a network of contractors it is possible that similar difficult situations may appear only in some sites and not in others.

The moment in which a subcontractor registers the problem and realizes that it has occurred at other sites, without having been informed, is always delicate to manage.

Unfortunately, there is no single way to deal with this situation.

It helps a continuous technical discussion within the client on the state of the art of the investigation so that the exact moment is identified to provide communication within the network. This is, in my opinion, the only correct method.

Alerting sites without having a clear understanding of the problem could generate an unwarranted alarm.

How to Deal with Big Changes, from Both Sides

Situation similar to that of direct production, with the difference that what happens within one of the two companies, in addition to having employees as an interlocutor, must also be shared with the partner.

What can be the big financial changes:

(a) Transfer of ownership to a third company (whole or a specific branch), which may or may not be interested in continuing the tracer production activities
(b) Decision to downsize or even remove the radiotracer from the priority list

Cases (a) and (b), if there is no interest in continuing production, have a similar course. Unfortunately, as is the case for the employees involved, given the confidentiality of these operations, there is not always the time and the way to notify and share the subcontractor well in advance of the change.

After an initial analysis of an exclusively contractual type, if the level of collaboration between the companies is such as to justify it, the company management can assume the responsibility of anticipating the transaction to the counterparty, shortly in advance and in a strictly confidential manner.

First reactions can only be negative, but great opportunities can also arise from the way they are subsequently processed.

The party that decides is clearly at a disadvantage: regardless of the legal aspects, years of collaboration create very strong relationships between companies, even personal ones. There is also the will to close the operation as soon as possible, without aftermath of a legal nature.

This is the moment for the company that somehow 'suffers' the news to quickly process the news and to put forward counterproposals that, although not able to change the final decision, can at least create a 'buffer' condition to favour the development of other opportunities.

I am thinking, for example, of the possibility of requesting the free transfer of ownership of equipment previously financed by the client or of the possibility of continuing to carry out the production and distribution of the product on one's own account.

Situations that can obviously be different depending on the situation but that have a common denominator: negotiating, to get as much as possible rather than insisting on making the other party give up.

In case (a), when the new customer intends to continue production, the problem is to ensure that the subcontractor accepts the new situation while maintaining the same relationship of trust existing with the previous customer.

Situations can be difficult if the merged entity has a competitive relationship on other products with the subcontractor.

There are also 'emotional' components for the subcontractor, beyond mere commercial and economic aspects.

The feeling of having been 'betrayed' by the initial partner, for example, and not having been adequately informed of what was going on.

In this case, my experience tells me that the only possible action is to dedicate structured time to the explanation, and let the new client introduce themselves and define the ways in which to structure the new relationships. It is just a matter of time.

Synergies, Mutual Development and Loyalty

Synergies
For example, using the subcontractor as a supplier for the technological development of new products.

The subcontractor's knowledge of the level of requirements, expectations and 'way of working' of the client company is a great value, intangible but capable of speeding up subsequent projects.

Mutual Development
I have found that often companies that decide to use a subcontractor 'self-censor' themselves, with the fear of expecting too much and having too high standards.

In reality, the subcontractor, from these situations, could only derive advantages, impalpable from an economic point of view but significant in terms of know-how development.

Relating to high standards allows them to broaden their catchment area and aim to offer themselves to increasingly large international realities as well as to draw benefits, for example, during inspections by regulatory bodies.

It is not an easy message to understand.

I happened to have to deal with subcontractors worried about the time they would have to dedicate to the customer's inspections, in some cases (fortunately rare) I was also asked for financial compensation for each audit day.

Unfortunately, I found that these situations do not arise only with small realities, without previous experience, but also with developed realities with an international scope.

On the other hand, I met local production companies, with limited staff, enthusiastic to confront each other and without hesitation in allocating their resources.

Loyalty
In this text I often highlight what the problems may be in the relationship between the client and the subcontractor.

But things can also go very well between the parties and generate a virtuous relationship, which goes beyond the single Technology Transfer and the production for a single product. The parties may find reasons to share technical information (in some cases the customer could be a supplier of specific technology for PET), commercial information and establish a fruitful collaboration. In this context, real loyalty can be achieved, in the good sense of the term.

Chapter 7
Management of a PET Network

Abstract The author describes how to manage a PET network, the possible level of freedom of the manufacturing sites, the role of the local team and how to perform a financial analysis.

Keywords PET coordinator · Centralized or local control of manufacturing sites · Role of the local team · Business analysis

Setting Up Relationships, the Role of the PET Coordinator

A PET network includes multiple production sites that respond to a single client (in the case of outsourcing) or to a single property.

Within the same network, both 'owned' sites and third party sites can also operate simultaneously.

In all cases, and this is the topic we will address in this paragraph, the complexity is much greater than that of managing a single site.

Incidentally, for management I consider here the operational and financial aspects and not those, already strictly regulated, of quality and regulatory (which, however, from experience, cannot always be kept separate from the operational and financial aspects).

In a network, the need emerges to define and harmonize both communications to the various sites and the information returned from them and the related processing.

The first question that must be asked is the level of control we intend to apply on our sites, bearing in mind that greater control also requires more resources (and therefore costs), on both sides.

It is not strictly necessary, in my opinion, that we should imagine a rigorous control of the sites, at least in the initial stages of the development of the network.

Controlling in detail means knowing the process and having a clear view of what you actually want to control.

Knowledge, especially if the production involves new molecules, takes time.

It is therefore foreseeable that the two processes, knowledge and control, develop in parallel with the continuation of the collaboration.

The first relations between the parties, with the drafting of the letter of intent, normally involve only the top functions of the two companies, especially in the commercial part.

Almost all the company functions are already involved in the drafting of the contract and will then manage the operational part.

I speak mainly of Production, Quality Control, Regulatory Affairs and QA. It is an important moment because the first relationships and the opinion that people will form will influence all subsequent phases.

The common thread that is suggested is that of absolute transparency, even and above all if there have been negative episodes in other contexts both between the parties and in previous collaborations with different bodies.

It is useful to start from the "best practices" learned so far and explain the reasons for the operating and financial model that we intend to propose.

This approach must then continue throughout the collaboration.

In all the contracts that I have followed it is always indicated that the parties, once production has started, meet periodically with variable frequency (every six months or annually). Unfortunately, this commitment is not always respected.

The Figure of the PET Coordinator

Depending on the size of the network, this function can have a national or international dimension.

Their figure, I do not say this only because it was also my job, is essential and is the trait d'union between the 'Corporate' (the central structure of the client or owner) and the satellite production sites, whether they are owned or subcontractors.

They are responsible for collecting information and statistics related to production and distribution, processing and sharing them centrally and referring them, as regards best practices, to all operating sites.

The PET Coordinator is the direct reference for the functions of the client company that operate in the distribution area of each production site.

As a site contact, the PET Coordinator is usually the first contact for any need, not just operational.

It is useful that this figure is also coordinated by a financial analyst, especially in the case of production sites located in several countries and if the production of some of them is marketed in countries other than the place of production.

In the latter case, a supranational financial analysis, of which no local financial structure can have complete visibility, will allow us to keep track of the actual profitability of the sites. Normally, the role of PET Coordinator is covered by figures who have grown up within the PET world, for example QP or Site manager elevated to the role of national or international coordinators.

However, it is appropriate that the PET Coordinator refrains from the quite natural temptation to limit themselves to the technical and operational aspects (dose and batch reliability for example) and organizational aspects, more suited to their training and experience, but also and above all take care of a rigorous financial control of the sites.

The PET Coordinator will also be the company reference figure in the case of new commercial or production opportunities.

The commercial service, usually the first to detect opportunities in the area, will benefit enormously from the previous experience gained by the PET Coordinator.

Degrees of Freedom: Local or Centralized Control?

To what extent must the control of production realities be centralized and when is it better to entrust it to local realities?

There is no single answer, the choice depends on:

(a) Size of the production network, the number of sites and level of distribution of the same in different countries
(b) The presence of a company structure in the country in question
(c) Type of skills present in the area
(d) Degree of trust of the Corporate

Normally, the part entrusted to the local reality is the operational part of production management; for quality assurance and regulatory activities the local contribution can integrate but hardly completely replace the central contribution.

In my experience, the control is born centralized, perhaps identified with the first operational site. With the development of the network, support activities are also developed, for example, a central PET Planner figure who plays an interface role between the sites and the local Customer Services, if not directly with the diagnostic centres in the case of internal clinical studies or collaborations, with pharmaceutical companies that use the PET tracer for their clinical studies.

Over a certain number of production sites and with the increase in production volumes, if local organizational conditions allow, the Customer Service and the Commercial Service take control of the site's operational activities.

In the case of several production sites located throughout the country, their role is to sort the needs of customers according to the logistical conditions (greater or lesser distance from the production centre), the production capacity and of course according to the needs of the clinical centres.

An activity that requires specific knowledge of the territory and customers could hardly be carried out centrally.

The transition from centre to periphery requires the training of the local team, with insights into the contracts stipulated, the economic and logistic conditions of supply and the peculiarities of the PET tracer.

This coordination activity, combined with the development of production activities, could generate the need to modify the existing contracts to make them more suited to local needs, creating in my opinion a virtuous circle.

In the event that the production site is distributed over several countries, the need is created to establish a unique communication with it.

This activity can be carried out by the figure of the "PET Planner" who does not replace the responsibilities of the Customer Services of the individual countries in managing orders but harmonizes them in concert with the production site, in order to allow the definition of balanced production plans.

By balanced we mean an exploitation of at least 80% of production capacity and a supply schedule that, even if with some minimal adjustments, is able to meet the needs of all countries.

As I indicated earlier, the operational management of the sites, by its nature, is much more likely to be delegated to local functions than quality and regulatory activities, linked to different logics.

The contradiction could develop in those situations, which require, such as the management of production failures and complaints, a considerable detail of information in which the local Quality figures, if present, could provide valid support that, however, is not exploited as it is not previously involved in the management of the radiotracer.

My opinion is that widening the level of knowledge can always be an opportunity, even if by involving more actors the process becomes more complicated by requiring and effectively imposing the definition of an articulated communication system, which must be managed and controlled at central and peripheral level.

Is it possible to speak of trust between central and local functions that belong to the same company? In my opinion yes, this is a real problem.

Corporate functions, by definition, focus on centralizing and defining general processes that, however, cannot always be applied locally.

When this happens, one does not always have the intellectual honesty to admit the error of evaluation committed. The reaction is to imagine a lack of interest and motivation in the periphery, in general a lack of 'trust', in applying the rules already defined.

These situations are especially exacerbated when local functions, accustomed to managing business processes on already consolidated product portfolios, are not involved in the project strategies of the radiotracer.

It is therefore necessary, before reaching easy conclusions, that the Corporate devotes time to involve local functions, updating them on the stages of the various projects, in order to obtain their participation and a proactive approach in solving problems.

The Role of the Local Team in Relations with Subcontractors

The local team, depending on whether it is an international (for example, pan-European) or national contract, has a very important role in the management of the site, as it is presumed to have played in the choice of its strategic opportunity.

When the site becomes operational, it is the local team that must develop strong relationships with it, which can hardly be replaced by the Corporate.

The local team knows the area and the needs. It is up to themselves to define customer coverage areas and situations that require the most attention.

In pure contract form, in theory, we should only expect the site to make the product available on such a day and time.

The contract is defined well in advance, even years, compared to the actual production, and, especially as regards the days and times of production, the indication that is inserted is normally a general indication with reference to a minimum number of productions, since they usually constitute an economic obligation for the client.

The commercial needs and the production availability of the site, in the meantime, could have changed and what were the operational constraints at the time of the first agreements already exceeded.

In addition, from my experience, contractors, with rare exceptions, are pleased to be involved in commercial strategies.

They constitute, like the technical activities, a point of comparison, a challenge, which allows them to demonstrate to the client the reliability and seriousness of the company.

Not infrequently I have come across situations in which the subcontractor has proposed valid alternative commercial solutions.

The comparison is also an element of development for the client's local staff who learns about the tracer in more and more detail, involving not only the top management of the company but also the 'field' staff, who work in the various regions.

In the initial phase, the meetings between local officials of the client company and the subcontractor should be mediated by the Corporate figures who managed the project and the agreements, above all to avoid that the starting point is different from the vision set initially.

Subsequently, it is desirable that contacts are frequent and managed independently from the Corporate, even if within the contractual conditions.

At the end of the technology transfer, the site is able to meet the standard production needs, but it may be necessary to 'challenge' the production capacity in order to make it more compatible with local needs. This 'calibration' can and should be completed.

In the event that local legislation allows the production start-up of the site within a relatively short time from the completion of the technology transfer, it is desirable that this alignment of the site on the production capacities, requested by the local team, takes place before and during the technology transfer phases.

A very delicate situation to manage, having to mediate between the qualification activities (with their difficulties and their timing) and projecting oneself towards the operational phase.

Financial Analysis

Financial analysis, together with operational feasibility, is the fundamental part for choosing a subcontractor.

On the client's side, the points to be analysed are:

(a) A list of customers reachable by the subcontractor, frequency and the number of orders (possibly on a monthly basis).
(b) Estimated duration of supplies.
(c) Estimated sales prices of the product.
(d) Variables that could increase or decrease the demand of the aforementioned customers (for example, installation of new PETs, reimbursement of the drug).
(e) Any synergies with customers served by other subcontractors in the area who could benefit from additional supplies or alternative days of production.
(f) Opportunities in new territories that however require particular logistic solutions. In this case it is advisable not to include them in the financial analysis until the actual feasibility and costs of the proposed solutions have been verified.

It is not always possible to carry out a reliable business analysis.

For example, in the case of new tracers, the values provided by the commercial service could have an indicative meaning only, based on theoretical opportunities.

In this case it is appropriate to share the initial concerns also with the subcontractor, in order to be able to reduce, as far as possible, the initial production effort and adjust it according to actual needs.

The above points must be appropriately compared with the production costs.

Production costs consist of several variables:

(a) The presence or not on site of the equipment necessary for production
(b) Initial product validation costs
(c) Cost of the lot (value always present)
(d) Cost of raw materials (if supplied by the customer, otherwise they will be included in point c)
(e) Any 'fee' per dose, where 'fee' means the fixed value that is charged for each dose produced
(f) Any royalties on the sale of the product
(g) Maintenance cost (common cost in particular geographical areas, such as the US)

(a) This is certainly an element with an important impact.

If the tracer requires a particular synthesis or dispensing module and the site does not have one, the analysis of a possible purchase, installation (with related modification of the environments) and qualification can have a heavy impact on the project.

In this case, it is necessary to evaluate the investment in perspective, considering the possibility, for example, that the proposed solution may also favour a possible development of the subcontractor on other products.

The new equipment could be used for other tracers, other than the one being analysed, that the client or the subcontractor themselves could develop in the future.

In any case, the investment must find a justification, and it is highly probable that the client will have to bear part of the costs. If the conditions allow it, it may be worth testing the willingness of the subcontractor to distribute the costs for the client during the various phases of the project, ideally starting from the production batches. In a commercial project, the possibility of transferring costs when the possibility of having an economic return opens up for the client could constitute an undeniable advantage.

(b) The value can be variable depending on whether or not to provide a detailed validation package for the tracer. For already registered products this is usually not a problem.

Having already been approved by a regulatory body, it is likely that the specifications and analytical and production methods are well-defined and extremely reproducible.

In the case of new tracers, in the phase of clinical study or even preliminary to the same, they require an inevitable technological development on the production and quality control methods that will heavily affect the offer of the subcontractor.

(c) In the cost of the batch, the site includes the costs of raw materials (if not supplied by the customer), of personnel, depreciation and maintenance of equipment, cost of support functions (for example, management of production orders and logistics activities).

The price may vary depending on several factors:

1. Geographical location and relative cost of living. For example, in Northern Europe the value of the lot can even double or triple compared to the countries of Southern Europe.
2. Production times. In the case of products with reduced synthesis times and extremely rapid quality control methods, it will be easier for the CMO to allocate the production of other tracers on the same day and, consequently, to propose an advantageous offer for the customer.
3. Commitment of the client. The more it requires a high number of batches per period of time, committing to them (therefore paying them a priori, assuming the risk that there may be fewer requests than those foreseen) the more the subcontractor, having the guarantee of production continuity, is in the conditions to reduce the price of the batch. Conversely, it will be higher if the client does not intend to engage in the productions.

4. The number of tracers to be developed. A business deal that considers more than one product, even over a large timeframe, is more likely to deliver an advantageous offer.
5. Competition with other products made by the subcontractor.

If the CMO has few free production intervals due to an already consistent production rate, the insertion of a new tracer will necessarily have to compete with those already present. This is the most difficult situation, with less room for negotiation, as the batch value of our tracer inevitably has to compare with the other tracers in the CMO portfolio.

(d) Cost of raw materials. If the client provides raw materials for the synthesis and the approach with the CMO is purely outsourced, there is obviously no interest on the part of the client in making excessive profits from the sale of the same.

The subcontractor, in fact, includes the cost of raw materials within the batch price. Each change in the price of raw materials leads to a change in the price of the batch.

(e) The 'fee per dose' is a value that is charged by the CMO to the customer for each dose produced or for each dose interval.

With this request, the CMO becomes a participant in the client's business, increasing its revenues as a function of the expansion of the market and the relative increase in the required doses.

The per dose fee can be an opportunity to share commercial risks with the CMO and to try to keep the batch value at a low level.

In my opinion it is an excellent solution in the case of new markets where it is difficult to predict the real sales volumes.

However, this formula has a limitation and is inherent in the sharing of risk.

For example, the CMO may not approve the production of batches for limited volumes of doses which the client may consider necessary for strategic reasons in the area.

The logic of compensating only the batch, on the other hand, does not give rise to any doubts, as the CMO could theoretically not be interested in the number of doses produced. I say theoretical because a good CMO has all the interest in monitoring the utilization of the lots to verify the commitment and the actual will by the client in the development of the radiotracer.

It is necessary to evaluate the choice of the fee also according to the risk that the sale price of the dose could undergo variations. In the case of price increases, a fixed fee leads to economic advantages for the client; in the opposite case it obviously constitutes a problem. The fees may have a different value depending on the number of doses produced.

For example, a solution that is often used involves setting the price of the batch with a minimum number of doses already inside.

Beyond this number, fees are applied, which may have a lower value as the number of doses increases.

(f) Royalties. Unlike the fee, which is a fixed value, in the royalty the CMO requires a fixed percentage of the price of the dose sold.

The percentage can be applied:

1. On customer sales.
2. On sales from which transport costs have already been subtracted (normally referred to as the 'net selling price').
3. On the sales to which the transport costs and the costs that the customer undertakes for the marketing of the product have been subtracted (for example, for the personnel of the commercial and logistic functions).

Normally, the formulas applied are (1) and (2). Formula (3) is difficult to accept by the CMO, also due to the actual difficulty of demonstrating, or rather of allocating the customer's internal costs to the specific product.

In this case, as in the fee (point (e) above), the CMO 'enters' the client's business, drawing more benefit, than in the fee model, from any commercial efforts to increase the sales value of the tracer.

Final Greeting

At the end of the reading, together with the reader, allow me to pull the strings of the key points that I was able to share in the various chapters and which I hope to be able to convey.

To begin with the concept of complexity of PET production.

Although, of course, the ultimate goal is to produce the radiotracer, many skills develop around it, all equally important, even if at first sight not directly connected with production (I mentioned, for example, the Customer Service or the quality functions and regulatory).

Not approaching production as a team but as an activity reserved only for the technical department is a serious mistake.

Expanding the audience of those who know the product well, even in its technical aspects, is essential in order to ensure a truly effective exploitation of production capacity and a clear vision on the objectives that the company can really pursue.

In light of the small size of the manufacturing site, the production team must also be educated on what happens 'outside'.

Another point is that of the automation of processes, which can be a real pitfall for the company.

There are no processes, at least in PET, that can do without humans despite the confinement of production and the now increasingly high presence of automatic robots and their management software.

Beyond the fact that, as I explained, complexity risks dazzling and stimulating further complexity, the human being and their serenity of judgement - made up of shifts, adequate environments and defined and agreed processes in which everyone can feel protagonist - must remain at the centre of the life of the manufacturing site.

I allowed myself, I say permission because I am aware of how difficult it is in reality, even to stress several times how it is necessary to try to align production shifts with the quality of life of employees.

A. Pecorale, *Essence of the PET Radiopharmaceutical Business*, SpringerBriefs in Business, https://doi.org/10.1007/978-3-030-97937-9

Striving in this direction leads to benefits for the company, because having the ability to retain employees reduces the turnover and efforts for costly continuous training and facilitates the company in attracting talent.

I have always tried to 'listen' to the corridors, perhaps also because, as I mentioned, I had a first forward-looking manager who demanded that I live only with 'the workers' for two years.

What happens in the walls of a manufacturing site, how the operators are considered and even the economic treatments, are part of a popular 'vulgate' of those who work in the sector and that goes beyond the companies themselves.

It would be interesting to understand how this information is transferred, but we have seen in the text that there are many opportunities for contact between PET companies, precisely because they are limited in number.

We have mentioned how to try to make production profitable. There are no magic formulas but only a joint work that sees together the product and who will have the task of managing its marketing.

We have analysed the differences between direct production and subcontracting and I think I can say that for both there is the exact same management complexity.

Contracting is not, as is often thought, the easiest way, and we do not think that it is possible to transfer the commercial or production risk to a third party just because it is not wanted, even temporarily, to assume it directly. Sooner or later the consequences will be paid.

The sharing of corporate strategies at all levels is also fundamental, including in the relationship with the CMOs.

Maintaining continuous contact between the various internal functions of the company and with the CMOs is the only way to be able to see any 'curves' in advance and perhaps better deal with the difficult situations that inevitably arise.

Having said that, allow me to greet and thank the reader who has had the patience to read this text to the end.

I am aware that some points could have been better developed, or that the addition of graphs and tables would have allowed a detailed analysis.

But my goal, as I specified at the beginning, was not to draw up a vademecum but only to align general reflections. If they find some interest, I do not exclude that there may be further investigations.

I have tried, with this book, to empathize and recognize the efforts of the unknown world of operators and technicians that, facing enormously technical and logistic issues, are really spending their life to guarantee the regular supply of radiotracers to the hospitals.

Thank you for any comments or criticisms that, like everything that has happened to me so far in my professional life and not, will help me improve.

Glossary

Airport handling Administrative and cargo handling activities performed within an airport.

Back-up Supply of the radiopharmaceutical agreed on the occasion of temporary interruptions of production due to planned or unplanned maintenance.

CMO (Contract Manufacturing Operation) Subcontractor.

Glove box Literally 'glove box' is a sealed container for handling instruments and substances in a confined environment completely separate from that in which the operator is.

Labelling Operation through which a radionuclide is inserted into the structure of the chosen drug in such a way that, after the administration of the radiopharmaceutical, the radiations emitted by it are detected by a radiation detector. In this way it is possible to evaluate the morphological structure or the physiological function of the organ.

PET Acronym for 'Positron Emission Tomography'. Nuclear Medicine diagnostic technique able to offer, with a high degree of precision, information on organ and tissue pathologies.

PET pharmaceutical manufacturing site Pharmaceutical manufacturing site specifically dedicated to the production of radiopharmaceuticals for PET diagnostics.

Pharmaceutical manufacturing site Structure that, following specific authorizations, is able to carry out all operations for the purchase of materials and products, Production, Quality Control, release, storage, distribution of medicines and related controls.

Procedural system The list of documents, reviewed and approved by the responsible company functions, which regulate all the activities of the Pharmaceutical Manufacturing site.

QA (Quality Assurance) Body that guarantees that the principles and standards of Good Manufacturing Practices (GMPs) are always applied consistently.

© The Author(s), under exclusive license to Springer Nature Switzerland AG 2022   81
A. Pecorale, *Essence of the PET Radiopharmaceutical Business*, SpringerBriefs in Business, https://doi.org/10.1007/978-3-030-97937-9

QP (Qualified Person) Responsible for ensuring that each batch has been manufactured and checked in compliance with laws in force in the Member State where certification takes place, following the requirements of the marketing authorisation (MA) and with Good Manufacturing Practice (GMP).

Radiation protection Discipline that studies methods to safeguard humans from the biological damage that radiation of any kind can cause.

Radioactive concentration Total radioactivity per volume unit (example MBq/mL).

SMF (Site Master File) Document prepared by the pharmaceutical manufacturer that contains specific information about the site's quality management policies and activities, the manufacturing and/or quality control of the pharmaceutical manufacturing operations performed.

SPECT Acronym for 'Single Photon Emission Computed Tomography'. Unlike PET, radioisotopes are used that do not emit positron, but gamma radiation directly.

VMP (Validation Master Plan) Document in which the key elements of the production site qualification and validation program are identified and documented.

References

Radiopharmaceuticals for Positron Emission Tomography, Gerhard Stöcklin, Victor W. Pike, 1993, Springer

La Qualità nella preparazione dei radiofarmaci, Giovanni Lucignani, Springer, 2011

Basics of PET Imaging, Physics, Chemistry, and Regulations, Gopal B. Saha, PhD, Springer, 2016

Quality in Nuclear Medicine, Andor W.J.M. Glaudemans, Jitze Medema, Annie K. van Zanten, Rudi A.J.O. Dierckx, 2017, Springer

Nuclear Medicine Textbook, Duccio Volterrani, Paola Anna Erba, Ignasi Carrió, H. William Strauss, Giuliano Mariani, 2019, Springer

Radiopharmaceutical Chemistry, Jason S. Lewis, Albert D. Windhorst, Brian M. Zeglis, 2019, Springer

Radiopharmaceuticals, Ferdinando Calabria, Orazio Schillaci, 2020, Springer

EudraLex - Volume 4 - Good Manufacturing Practice (GMP) guidelines

Printed in the United States
by Baker & Taylor Publisher Services